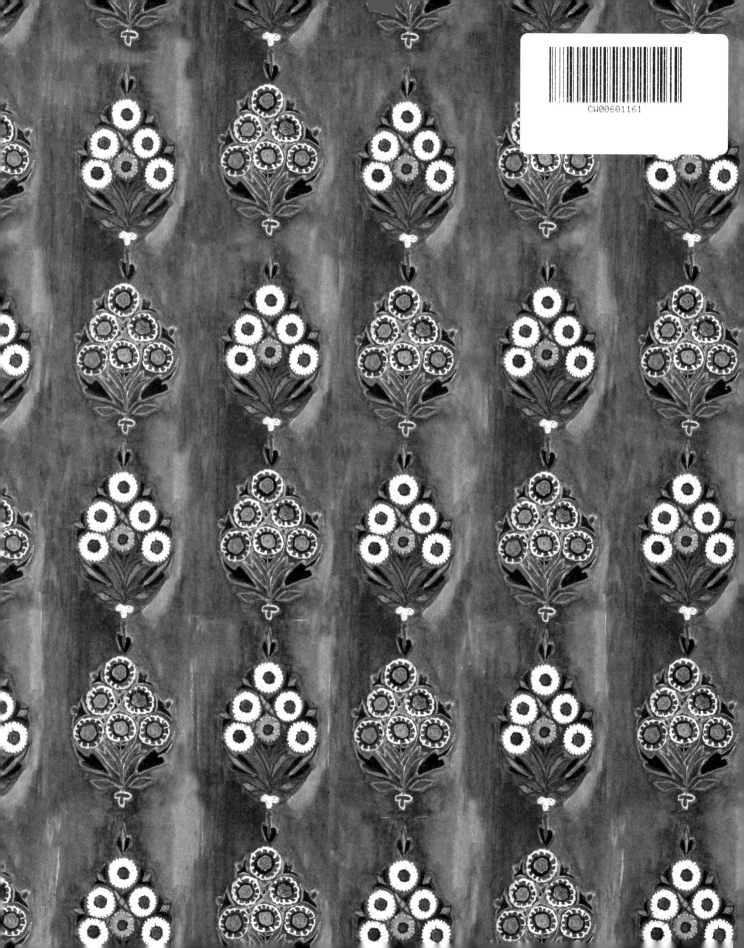

THE GOLDEN THREAD

With best
wishes
Lawen J Reudley
23/8/15

Undoubtedly Lorna Tresidder is an eminent artist & her colourfully illustrated book "The Golden Thread", vividly details the dress, colourful embroidery, customs & traditions which survive in remote communities of Kutch - a place apart - that are getting rapidly diluted. This then is a vibrant & timely record of the changes she has personally observed & which are inevitable over time, in every tradition bound society. In a way reading this book is to travel back & across time, offering a rich & detailed narration of a neglected people, their history culture & distinct identity.

PRAGMULJI III
Maharao of Kutch

THE GOLDEN THREAD

The disappearing world of Indian village culture

Lorna Tresidder

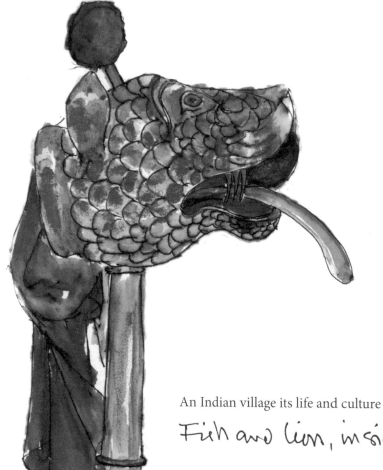

An Indian village its life and culture

Fish and lion, insignia Maharao of Kutch

Acknowledgements

Putting the book together has been engrossing, from writing it to painting the illustrations and designing the book. I am very appreciative to my many friends who have given their support and I am particularly indebted to the following for their generous help in putting the book together.

Maureen Zadow for her help and patience, Charles Metcalfe for his valuable suggestions, likewise Celia Fox and Inger John. David Taylor for composing the book for printing. Shri Jethi for taking me to see wrestling. The late Shri Gulbeg, headman to Dhordo village and his son, the present headman Miaw Gulbeg. Lastly Poppelie, Sifyer and Mzharuddin (referred to in my text by his shortened name Alladin), my guide to many events and Banni villages.

A sincere thank you to His Highness Shri Pragmulji, for information regarding the former kingdom, and to my children Justin, Thomasin and Tresidder, to whom I dedicate the book.

Published in Great Britain and India by
Indian Romance Publishing Ltd, London.
e-mail: info@indianromance.co.uk
www.indianromance.co.uk

ISBN 978-0-9928188-0-7

Printed and bound in India by Sonigraphics Mumbai

Contents

PAKISTAN

Sindh

Grea

The Kingdom of Kutch

Now part of the state of Gujarat, Kutch
was an independent kingdom from the
late 13th century until the partition
of India in 1948. Banni, where most of
the villages described in this book are
located, is an open tract of grassland,
traditionally occupied by wandering
herdsmen. Climatic and economic
pressures are affecting the grasslands,
causing villagers to drift to cities.

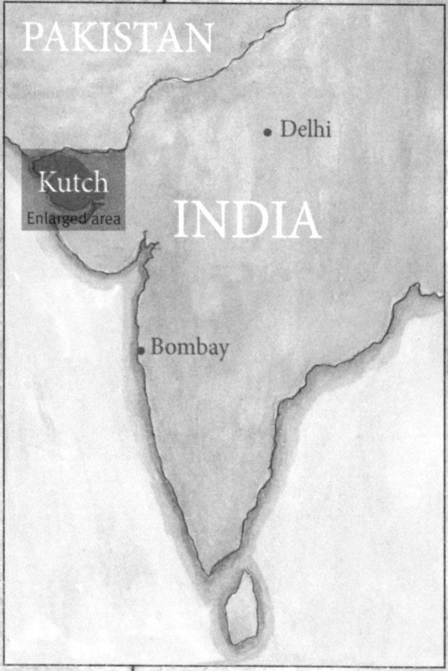

Mouth of
the Indus

PAKISTAN

• Delhi

Kutch
Enlarged area

INDIA

• Bombay

Arabian Sea

*A typical 12 manned Kutch vessel of the
19th Century, plying the waters down the
West Coast of India to Kerala, and Bombay.
These small craft also went across to Africa
and the Middle East. From Africa they
bought back glass beads used in the local
Kutch embroidery. They were also a great
plague to the English with their voracious
piracy.*

50km

Headman Miaw Hussein
wearing the traditional
Mutwa turbans. It is an
Ajrakch pint in natural
colours of indigo and madder

Foreword

Kutch, Cutch, Kachachh, Dhordo village.

I fell in love with India and its culture nearly forty years ago. I took a year's leave from my post and went to study Indian Textiles. Today, India is a changed place in many ways, but the exhilaration, energy and heightened awareness this love gives me in my daily life is as much a reality for me now as it was then.

The changes took place imperceptibly - that is, until about 1997, when a mixture of events combined to cause India to alter rapidly. Modern roads, the importation of modern cars, diesel engines instead of steam locomotives, and modern communications were all key factors for transformation. Now mobile phones and the internet are playing a major role in changing the village way of life. Television, now in many homes, is playing its part in the replacement of the traditional garments of both men and women for more Western fashions. Many customs and traditions are being lost and even visually India is different.

Before these ways of life disappear, I want to record some of my earlier experiences. Whilst looking generally at India, I am focusing my attention on the pocket of India which before Partition formed the Kingdom of Kutch. The kingdom ended with Partition and was renamed Kachach, covering the same land mass as the former kingdom. According to the present Maharao, Pragmati Singhi, Kutch was for many centuries spelt with a K with the English altering the K to a C (Cutch). However, his ancestor objected the C as it made the name spell 'cut' at the beginning and so it was altered back to the K. His Highness prefers that I use the historical name of Kutch, which is now once more commonly used.

Kutch forms almost a natural island. The people of Kutch have very distinctive dress, customs and unique traditions, which I was privileged to see and experience. Below the Great Rann of Kutch, which forms a natural partition between India and Pakistan, is where Dhordo village, the focus of this book, is situated. In 1975 the village was a remote and far-off place with no road to it. It lies at the extremity of the former kingdom.

The territory of the village and of the kingdom itself was difficult to reach, with the kingdom forming, by its own geography, a natural defence against other warring kingdoms. It was not properly surveyed until the Raj came. But when I first visited Kutch in 1975 maps were non-existent. Travelling was all done with the help of local knowledge.

Kutch is bounded by the Arabian Sea to the south, by Pakistan to the West, by the Great Salt Rann to the north and by the Little Rann to the East. At the junction of the Little Rann with mainland Gujarat, Kutch could be cut off by monsoon waters combining with the risen seawaters. If the monsoon fell in great volume, it would cause flooding, often with loss of life. In 1979 twice the usual volume of water fell in just two days, the suddenly swollen waters causing unprecedented flooding at Morvi with between 5,000 and 10,000 deaths. Because of this disaster a major engineering scheme was undertaken to avert a tragedy of this magnitude ever happening again. The excess waters are now taken off and bigger bridges have been built to span this junction for both road and rail traffic.

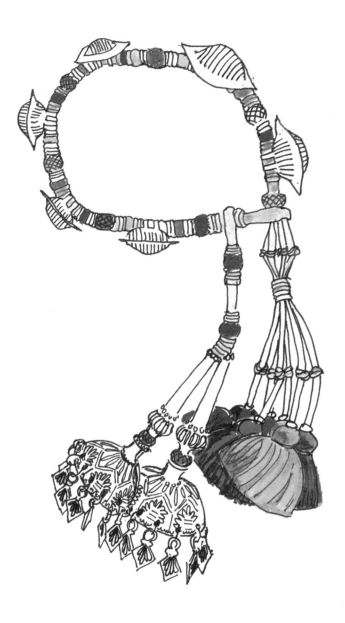

Arm bracelet, worn by a young girl above the elbow to stop the upper arm bangles falling down. As she grows and her arm increases in size the arm then holds the bangles in place. Now both traditions have gone.

FOREWORD

It can be seen that the natural geography of Kutch has given it all the aspects of an island and, through its natural separation and apartness, has forged over the centuries its own very individual personality and character.

The landmass of Kutch is 45,652 square kilometres, a quarter of the size of Gujarat. Without including either of the Ranns, the land is some 272 miles from East to West and 80 miles south to north, with the Tropic of Cancer passing through the middle of Kutch some ten miles above Bhuj, the capital of Kutch.

Running below the Great Salt Rann of Kutch is a stretch of grassland. In this region there are some forty-six villages which have earned their living by following pastoral pursuits. Dhordo village, the focus of my book, is one of them

Dhordo was at the time of my visit the premier village, its headman being a remarkable man called Shri Gullbeg. Through his hospitality, I came to know the customs and way of life of this village and the surrounding villages.

My visit to Kutch was the highlight of my sabbatical year in India. I went three times to stay in this picturesque village with its warm hospitable people. Over the following forty years I have visited it many times. I have seen its children grow up and be married.

Village life, which was formerly the kernel and centre of Indian life, now stands on the brink of destruction, its purity of tradition and customs already being eroded. This book shows the changes I have observed and forms a record of it as it is today, before it is further engulfed into a commonality. I recognise this village as having something precious, which I would greatly regret to see disappearing, although I fear for it. I set out to encompass some of its culture and traditions and, above all, to record the heart of the village, with people's lives closely linked in day-by-day kinship and custom.

In order to give the setting to the village and its place within the Kingdom of Kutch, from which its culture has been shaped and distilled, I trace the villagers' history back to when, as migratory people, they were given permission by the Maharao of Kutch to settle in Banni. The capital of Kutch is Bhuj (sixty five miles from the village). Bhuj has for many hundreds of years been not only the capital but also the principality where the royal family ruled, lived and built their various palaces over the centuries. I have therefore included a chapter showing some of the splendid architecture of the palaces of Kutch, some of the royal artefacts, court embroidery and a chapter on the religious stone carvings called Pallia, which are unique to Kutch.

All these topics are of great interest. Kutch abounds in so much that it is has been difficult to confine the text. What I have selected allows a strong contrast to be shown between the village, its setting within the former kingdom, and some of the kingdom's rich, complex and diverse culture.

Time off for the border
patrol camels.

I have combined writing with my paintings and drawings. Most of the artwork has been recently executed, but there are some very relevant drawings made on my first visit, and some of my original notes have been used.

In some parts, my sketchbook has been reproduced with my hand-written notes. I have also put in some diary entries, which I hope will provide the reader with a picture of my daily life and the life of the village.

An important theme of the book is the embroidery which the women in all the Banni villages produced. In 1975, when I first visited the village, women and girls from the age of eight were all to be seen embroidering for themselves and for their dowries. This skill and individuality within the village communities is disappearing and the embroidery is now too often adulterated. This has been brought about predominantly by commercial interests from outside, which now employ many women throughout the Banni villages. This has given the women extra rupees, at the cost of their own embroidery, learned from oral tradition, being neglected and forgotten.

The title for my book, "The Golden Thread", came from observing the village embroidery. I found that the beautiful gold and silver laid thread-work was common to all the villages. In appendix 3 you will find the working drawings of the main stitches used in Banni embroidery.

Previous travellers to India should find my book interesting, as it takes a close look at aspects of Indian village life and customs. It should bring to attention the value of taking time to sit and to look and observe. This applies to a first-time traveller as well. Though India is changing, it is still a very rewarding country to travel in, and Kutch remains for me the most individual cultural treasure.

The strong overall memory of my first visit to the village was that I felt as near to heaven as I would ever be on this earth. I returned to Bhuj this winter 2009 from my second longest visit to the village since 1975, and I felt as though I was emerging from a dream. It was certainly from another reality, and again I had the same feelings as on my first visit.

The impressions of my experiences remain rich and precious. I wish to share some of this with you.

Grasslands of Banni

Dhardo Village Banni

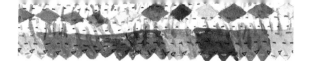

Chapter 1

Arriving in India

How in 1975, did I, a Western woman with three young children, arrive in a remote village in India? And this same question and answer would lead to my travelling extensively in India by train, jeep, rickshaw and Government car, to sleeping in village tents and maharajahs' palaces, to crossing the dust-covered desert of Banni to remote villages, and to lifelong, deeply-treasured friendships. I would also to be privileged to study and experience the intricate and beautiful embroidery used in the richly-worked village garments, domestic items, and quilts and distinctive forms of dress. This was my sabbatical leave.

1975 was well before the days of package tours and international holidays and travel, and here I was, at the age of thirty-seven, with my three children of eleven, nine, and seven, stepping out onto the aircraft steps, to descend into the full, humid heat of Bombay at the time of the monsoon. Looking back over the distance of years, I wonder at myself. I believe my very lack of knowledge and innocence of travel gave me a blank, wonderful sheet to fill with totally new impressions, relationships and truly memorable adventures.

We were to be met by a taxi which was taking us to Poona, where we were to stay initially with a doctor's family. First, however, I had to deal with endless paperwork for immigration, as there were no computers to record such information at this time. On final completion of this we were besieged by porters. Each child had their own suitcase and had packed it so they could manage to carry it for themselves. I was not to know that in India there are porters everywhere, and that they compete for work. Mayhem erupted as different porters captured their booty; in this case my children's suitcases, piling them on their heads and speeding off with them. I hastily got the children together and we flew after them, weaving our way through the crowds to catch up with the porters and our possessions.

On our emergence from the safety of the airport we were met with the full onslaught of India. A barrage of noise and people assailed us on every side, clamouring for our attention.

At last, to our relief, we found a taxi driver with a card bearing my name. By now, it was growing dark and, from the interior of the taxi in the stifling heat, I found it difficult to make sense of my surroundings. In the gloom, isolated single light bulbs or kerosene lamps illuminated small, immediate areas. All the colours were in the black range, with dark wrapped figures everywhere, many in booths or what looked like cupboards, others standing beside carts. Small hands were being thrust through the windows of the taxi. There were throngs of people in such volume as I had never experienced and was totally unprepared for. Many by their ragged appearance demonstrated their poverty. It was a Bombay version of Dickens's East-End of London in the 19th Century.

Later, as I settled into India, I came to understand what I then saw. The booths were bazaars and the people in them were often seated cross-legged, selling anything from dried goods to vegetables. At regular intervals there would be a paan walla sitting cross-legged on his waist-high shelf, in his small booth of a cupboard, with his condiments and leaves spread around him. The paan leaves were always decoratively arranged in neat circles with the pointed end of the leaf turned outwards. The paan walla would smear a leaf with a mixture of lime, tobacco, spices and betel nut, wrap it tightly on itself and hand it to his customer. Many poor people took it to stave off hunger. Now this very common sight has largely gone, although sometimes paan can be found at weddings or celebrations, with the odd walla selling it on the street.

In the following chapters many of the changes will be seen, and in the history chapter later I look at the rich heritage of textiles and embroidery coming to the Western world from Kutch. But now I am concerned with getting you, my reader, to Dhordo village.

Previous page: group of Rabbaries conversing

Above: a gift given to Mrs Gulbeg from her future husband, made by a Pakistan craftsman before Partition. Within the amulets are written texts for good health and good wishes, and endearments given to a lass by her sweetheart.

When I had applied for my sabbatical leave to study Indian Textiles (I was Senior Lecturer in charge of Embroidery in the Fashion and Textiles Department of Liverpool Polytechnic, now John Moores University), I had written to both Cottage Industries and All Indian Handicrafts and, although they had not helped in my achieving my sabbatical year, once I was in India they could not have been more helpful.

After my children and I had spent some two weeks with the doctor's family we moved to a small flat near the centre of Poona and, the children having started at their schools, I decided to begin my studies. I contacted All India Handicrafts, and Cottage Industries, and I made several visits to them respectively in Bombay. They noted that my special interest was embroidery.

Cottage Industries helped me plan itineraries for study tours to see certain textiles, and one was a three-week tour outlined for a visit to the western part of Gujarat, where I would see an abundance of embroidery, plus other textile crafts.

My children were enrolled as boarders for this period, and after many days spent at the train station I succeeded in obtaining my tickets first to Bombay, then to Ahmedabad and next for the overnight train journey to Bhuj. In Ahmedabad I met another representative of Cottage Industries, who in turn gave me letters of introduction to the DDO (District Development Office) and the Circuit House in Bhuj, where I would be allowed to stay.

The letter of introduction was key to my experiencing and meeting so many diverse people who were not only interesting but also helped me gain rich information. This totally invaluable network opened many unexpected doors and gave me introductions to people from villagers to Maharajahs whom I value as my friends today.

An illustration or example of this chain of introductions would be Digvijay Singh, then the Raj Kumar of Wankaneer, introducing me to the Maharajah of Poshina, who in turn introduced me to Sunita and Love her husband. I have remained firm friends with all these people and in particular with Sunita and her family. We have watched both her family and mine grow up be married and have their own families.

Having obtained my letters of introduction and being briefed on what I might expect to see in Bhuj and in the Kutch area, I was taken to the station in Ahmedabad for the last leg of my journey down to Bhuj, and my sleeper found for me. On my thanking my escort, he said, as so many people said at this time, "It is my duty". That phrase is very memorable as it so clearly illustrates the unbounded courtesy and hospitality of India at this time. Now, you seldom hear it.

In 1975 all the trains were pulled by steam engines. They had wonderful, huge engines pulling up to thirty coaches. The sound of the engine, the hooting, the hissing steam, and the flag-waving from the guards to see us off, gave me a feeling of being back in my childhood.

Handsome herdsman wearing his best
Ajrakh print attending a livestock show.

Poppetie churning butter.
She rotates the paddle by
pulling the string to and fro,
the paddle being secured to a
fixture on the wall.

There was at that time no air-conditioning in either first or second class. I was in the second class. The sleeper coach had metal-barred, glass-less windows, with rows of metal-framed and wooden-slatted bunks in tiers of three. There was a central communicating corridor down the length of the carriage, with a foot lavatory at one end. The other occupants were women in saris and men in both dhotis and Western trousers, shirts and jackets. I must have gone to sleep, as when I woke up the compartment was filled with quite different people.

I am not sure who was the most curious. Clearly, I was the only white woman they had ever seen and I for my part had never seen such exotically and unexplainably dressed people. We all stared unabashedly at each other. As none of us could communicate by language, we shared some food. I gave them some sweets and they gave me samosas and different namkin (small fancy biscuits). The chai walla (tea man) came round and served us chai in unglazed, simply fired, small pottery cups. I noticed they all threw their cups out of the window. So I did the same.

Now the potter's skill is no longer required, as plastic cups are used. Unfortunately, these are not biodegradable, but are nevertheless still thrown from the train, where they blow about and become permanent litter in the countryside which the train passes through. Surely it would be better to have the delight of the potter's cup and for the potter still to have his job?

In 1975 India was innocent of plastic. It was litter-free as everything was lower degradable, with the wandering cow or pig eating everything. Such a contrast to the plastic litter-strewn India of today.

I arrived in the early morning at Gandhidham station, which is the terminus, so all the passengers got down. I along with many others had to catch a bus. I was going to Bhuj.

The appearance of the crowd was so arresting and distinctive in their costume and so different from what you will see today that I will describe them. First, the smiling faces of the men and women displayed teeth - but teeth which made the smile menacing, as their teeth seemed to be sharpened or pointed as fangs. Many of the women wore huge,

Gold work embroidery

single, ivory bracelets on one wrist, about four inches long and the full width of the elephant tusk. The bracelet was often rouged and fitted the wrist snugly, with its outer edge carved to a deep curve, making the circumference slender in the middle, rather like a dumbbell. These women wore dark, long shawls over their heads, black, ankle-length, full-gathered skirts and black blouses with rich glittering embroidery. Many women had tattoos on their arms and throats. Luckily everybody seemed as fascinated by me as I most certainly was by them, and I realised it would be all right to make some overtures. I asked to see one woman's tattoos and found that one of them was of an iron with a lead and plug on the end and another was of a radio.

The men, in contrast to the women's totally black outfits, wore white. They had a short, tightly-fitted bodice ending in the middle of the chest and, from this to the waist, cloth was pleated into it. The bodice held so many pleats that it made it fan out, giving it a frill-like aspect. Into this yoke were fitted skin-tight sleeves made much longer than the arm and forced up to make many wrinkles *(see illustration p 68)*. This top was worn over skin-tight trousers. The trousers, like the sleeves, were longer than the leg and were worn deliberately with as many tight wrinkles as could be got. The trouser length was at least fourteen inches longer than the length of the leg. The men's heads were wound with large, white turbans, while their ears were studded with gold earrings. Many of the men sported big curled moustaches and some wore beards of biblical proportions.

Other women were dressed in brightly coloured full skirts and blouses, which were mostly green with embroidered roundels on each breast, accompanied by brightly patterned head coverings *(see illustration*

page 129). Thin, ivory bracelets followed in procession from the wrist up to the top of the arm. Every woman's garments shone and danced.

I was later able to identify all the people that I saw according to their various castes and communities. Now, one will never see such an arresting sight, the traditional garments donating a further handsomeness and comeliness to the men and women. Only possibly at a wedding or festival, or a display put on for groups of tourists, will one now see something of this past glory.

I learnt afterwards that the appearance of the sharpened teeth was caused by excessive eating of betel nut, which had so stained and blackened the gums at the edges that it resulted in the rather ferocious animal-look it gave to the face when the person smiled. I also came to know the art

Tonga or ghari — the mode of transport in Bhuj in 1975. Now not seen.

The sweet maker at Birendira

of spitting, a consequence of chewing betel nut; great gobs would hit the ground and streaks of discoloured red spit festooned many walls in towns and villages at this time.

The ivory bracelet fits the wrist so well because it is put on when the girl is in her early teens and, as the wrist grows, the bracelet is held in place, and at the time of her marriage the bracelet is rouged with dye. Nowadays, the ivory has been replaced with plastic, or the bracelet is not worn at all. The black-clad lady was the female to the white-clad male, and they belonged to the Rabbari and Ahir communities. I always see them as being the negative to the other's positive.

Tattoos were widely worn then but now the practice has stopped. I saw many women with tattoos (although men did not wear them). The designs were mostly in a series of dots rather like dominoes. I only found this custom in some communities, the dotted tattoos often being on the neck and throat. Those I have described like the iron and the radio were chosen because they were desirable objects. Possibly they were the nearest the woman ever came to possessing them.

In 1975 everyone in Kutch wore their own style of dress. Now it is occasionally glimpsed when older women (who still wear their community or caste's dress) come from their village into the bazaar in Bhuj - which is still an excellent place to observe and find some of these wonderfully-dressed people on their daily errands and transactions. But mostly the traditional dress has been sold to the merchant or is only taken out at times of celebration. Today, the traveller in Bhuj will no longer have such glorious visions on every side, and no-one will be stared at as I was, and as I indeed stared at others. Nor will the red spit of the betel nut sail past you.

I climbed up the steep, metal stairs of the bus travelling to Bhuj, and was lucky enough to secure a seat. From where I sat I could see the Hindu bus driver making the daily ritual of his prayers (puja). On his dashboard he had a plastic idol of Lord Krishna, whom he was worshipping. Lord Krishna is very favoured in Kutch as he was born in Gujarat, of which Kutch now forms a part. The driver lit joss sticks and swept them round his idol, before placing them in a holder to burn in front of it. He then hung a garland of freshly strung marigolds around it. Above the windscreen was another big poster picture of Lord Krishna.

This ritual was commonly performed every day by lorry drivers and bus drivers and in most homes, each person worshipping the god of their choice. Over the years, I have ridden in cars and buses and seen some memorable idols. One remarkable one was an idol of Ganeshe, the Elephant God. At nightfall, when the driver switched on his car lights, Ganeshe lit up and flashed from red to blue during the whole journey. I do miss it, the ritual and daily honouring of the driver's personal god and the smell of the joss sticks.

On this occasion, the bus finally set off when nobody else could be crammed in either on the roof or inside. A more colourful bus load it would be hard to find. Every passenger had masses of baggage, which ranged from newspaper, string-wrapped parcels to cloth-embroidered bags, sacks, and cloth shopping bags. It was a struggle to maintain enough space to sit on and enough room to shuffle one's feet around in.

Although being fascinated by all my fellow passengers, after being trodden on and buffeted in general, I was pleased to get out of the suffocating press of people and find my way to the Circuit House. I finally received directions and climbed into a horse-drawn tonga, not dissimilar to a pony trap. I was not sure if the horse would survive the journey, as it was so thin. This was the only form of transport then, but now the horse has been replaced by the polluting auto-rickshaw.

I arrived at the Circuit House to find I had lost my letters. This had happened when I had taken them out to ask for directions. I sat down to collect myself and work out what to do. Then I was told someone was asking for me. It was Prasad, the District Development Officer. The man from whom I had asked the way had picked my letters up and seen the DDO's name, and as Prasad was a man of importance he had taken my letters to him. Prasad found my letter to be something out of the ordinary and had stepped over from his Government office, which was adjacent to the Circuit House, to meet me. He insisted I come to stay with himself and his wife, Annie.

I had a very enjoyable visit staying with them. Annie was the Collector (Collector of Taxes). India believes in promoting bright young people and giving them responsible roles early. Annie and Prasad were, like me, in their thirties, and both have subsequently had very distinguished careers in the Indian Civil Service.

It is an integral part of a District Developments Officer's job to know each and every village and all the textile crafts or pursuits of the people in his district. Prasad, with his experience, assigned to me a Government car, a driver, and an interpreter, a Mr Davi, and made out a programme, sending me on visits throughout Kutch. Mr Davi came with me on all the visits, a nondescript man who tolerated the villagers but who felt he was above them in his middle-class home in Bhuj, where he and his sari-clad wife and family lived.

I visited all the most important artists and craftsmen in each and every craft. The artist craftsmen and women were all family businesses, and today I still know the same craftsmen and women and their successive family members working in the same craft.

One of these families who are still good friends are the Ajrakh (vegetable dye block prints) printers at Damadka. On my first visit, they were fully employed printing the different fabrics each community then wore in Kutch. As the traditional fabrics are now mostly just worn for celebrations, they have changed their emphasis and now supply fabrics for the export market and for the different outlets in India, items such as bed-sheets, tablecloths and table mats and dress fabrics.

Ajrakh is a craft going back hundreds of years with fabric being found at Fostat in Egypt, examples of which can be found at the Ashmolean Museum in Oxford. The examples closely match the present-day designs.

Ajrakh is Arab/Persian in origin, coming from the word Azrak meaning "blue". Blue refers to the predominating colour, which was indigo blue, especially in the original textiles.

Harijan girl wearing her traditional out fit

Ajrakh block printing

This page is about the block prints that all the menfolk in the villages in Banni wear - and which you will see referred to in many images throughout the book.

Ajrakh is a fabric made by printing with carved wooden blocks using vegetable dyes on cotton. The colours used and worn by the Banni villagers are traditionally red alizarin or madder and blue indigo on a natural background. Master craftsmen are so skilled that they can print a fabric with a perfect registration on both sides of the cloth.

In its traditional setting, Ajrakh has been an expression of a particular way of life, which is fast being eroded by the accelerated forces of

Block pinter
Dhamadka

26

change. In the past and in 1975 the market was predictable; the Khatris (block printers, and I am talking about the block printers at Dhamadka and referring to information given to me by them) had immediate payment for their goods from the Maldhari herdsmen of Banni who were their customers. Ghee was always made by the herdsman households and sold at local markets so they had cash to pay them. The Khatri craftsman would put a bundle of fabrics on his shoulder and set out on well-established routes to hawk his wares, going to each household and village in a rotation of four months. In the marriage season, when more goods were in demand, a camel would be hired for a quicker and longer trip to the villages.

Process of block printing

I am describing the craft here in simple steps. I have only illustrated five steps, but there are seven stages as described below.

1 The fabric is prepared ready to receive the printing. To prepare the cloth it is first washed very thoroughly to remove any starch and impurities. The cloth is then dipped in a solution made with ground myrobalan which is rather like an oak gall and comes from the Terminalia Chebula tree found in India, Nepal, Thailand, and Burma. It gives the cloth a gently buttery colour - or teal as shown here - and works perfectly with both alizarin and indigo. However, its importance lies in the fact that it is a tannin based mordant (dye fixing). The tannin in myrobalan permits absorption of alizarin and iron acetate in the dying process. The wet cloth is spread to dry and when dry once again the process is repeated.

2 The cloth printed with iron mordant. Made traditionally from soaking horseshoes or nails in jaggery, (sugar cane) this deepens the shade, in this case deepening the indigo

3 The cloth printed with alum mordant. This deepens and fixes the alizarin.

4 Dyed in alizarin dye.

5 Not shown here. Printed with mud resist (consists of mud, lime, gum arabic and wheat flour to reserve the parts not to be dyed).

6 Not shown here. Fabric dyed in an indigo pit.

7 The final textile after washing.

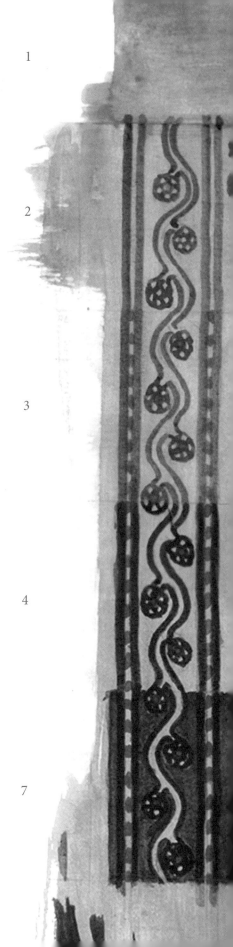

1

2

3

4

7

Models of the important maritime vessels used in Kutch.

Above: four-manned boat used for carrying goods from port to port in Kutch and as far down as Bombay.

Right: small craft for local fishing.

Below: a swift twelve-manned vessel trading down the length of the eastern side of India and across to the Middle East and the African coast. The men were able seamen and found easy plunder by turning pirate.

Opposite page: the little craft Lord Krishna is said to have used in Kutch.

Kutch is bounded by the Arabian Sea all along its southern edge, and has since ancient times boasted a hearty seafaring history: from earliest times, Kutch cloth has been one of its important cargoes, widely exported from her many sea ports to the East coast of Africa and to the middle-eastern countries.

I visited several villages around Bhuj, which also held important and distinctive communities, the most important being the Rabbarie and the Ahir communities, each producing distinctive embroidery work.

I understood that the villages fringing the great Rann of Kutch were inhabited by people who produced a diversity of embroideries, but to go to this area I had to obtain special permission. This took the form of written permission from the Government civil service department. This was a permit not only to visit but to stay in Dhordo village. It took three days, and if I had not known Prasad I doubt if I would have obtained permission to stay. It was, and still is, a sensitive area. Dhordo lies next to the Rann, which forms the natural barrier or frontier between India and Pakistan.

I no longer have my original permit from 1975, but to my joy I found my permit of 1985, when things were not so much different in the civil service. This hand-written permit had to do the round of different offices, each section writing its report. When every person has written his item, the permit is then placed in a folder and delivered by a servant to another person. This process is repeated, and so on, so you can see how long this all takes. Finally, I was personally interviewed by the superintendent of police, who then signed my permit and gave it to me.

I was now ready to set out on my journey to Dhordo village.

Chapter 2

Dhordo and the villages of Banni

I had taken the advice of Prasad, the District Development Officer, to visit the villages in Banni which are below the Great Rann. He recommended that I should go to the village of Dhordo to ask for help from the headman, Shri Gulbeg. Gulbeg was very knowledgeable about the area as he served the forty six villages of Banni as their headman. He knew the different communities and the embroideries that each village produced. Prasad felt, too, that I would be welcome to stay in Dhordo.

There was no way of requesting Mr Gulbeg's permission as there was no telephone service to the village. I always remember at this time in India that the unexpected guest was always "the honoured guest". Due to bad communications all over India at this time this was a frequent occurrence and a very frequent expression. The hospitality I encountered was without exception truly exceptional all over India.

I travelled in Prasad's own Government car, the big version of the Hindustan Ambassador, on the bonnet of which was the furled, sheathed flag used for formal occasions. To get to the village of Dhordo, my driver, guide and I first travelled from Bhuj, the capital of Kutch, by the single-track surfaced road which went up to Khavda: the last outpost facing the Pakistan border.

We travelled for some forty five miles, which took us to the village of Birendira, where we stopped to take tea and where I had my first taste of a special sweet made from buffalo milk. It is made over an open fire in a large, shallow-dished pan, some three feet in width. The hot milk is paddled to and fro until the milk gradually becomes solid. I was given some straight from the fire, and it was like eating delicious, warm, molten fudge. I took a supply for us, which was weighed and carefully packed in neatly folded newspaper and laced with white thread going round it many times in all directions.

We left Birendira, but after travelling only a hundred yards my driver abruptly deviated from the road, turning the wheel sharply left, so that the car descended onto the semi-desert of Banni. Immediately, the car filled with a fine, soft earth, like sand but composed of topsoil which had dried out and become powder. The windows of the car had brocade curtains held taut, top and

bottom, by plastic-coated wire springs. Whilst these curtains gave our car style and prestige and, when drawn, some protection against sunlight, they were totally ineffective against the fine soil of Banni. This clouded the air as it gradually filtered in, giving a fine covering to every surface.

As the car moved on, a long plume of dust rose up behind us and streamed like jet smoke over the parched land. In its slowness to settle once more, it marked the direction of our journey for many miles over this ancient landscape.

We travelled through a featureless countryside, which the hand of man has lain lightly on. Above was a blue and immense sky and, below, a dun-coloured landscape ruffled by eddies of wind and new dustings of soil. Bone-hard ridges and ruts, which we came upon from time to time, were the only signs of other people and vehicles having passed that way. These vehicles would have impressed their tracks onto the wet earth when the soil had become heavy clay with the monsoon. Travelling over these indentations stretched our car's suspension to its limit, rocking the car to and fro, so that we were pleased to return to the dust of the flat plain

The landscape was relieved by the odd, scrub acacia tree and now and again by clusters of thatched roofs peeping above the scrub. You could get lost and perish in this desolate landscape, and yet it pleased me.

Previous page: Hulbai wearing the Mutwa traditional costume.

Above: shoes worn by all Banni village women in 1975. Dyed green leather with silver and plastic strands interlaced in the leather.

Right: Nanima wearing the Mutwa traditional dress.

I quickly learnt to be on the alert when we passed close to the acacia's long slim branches with their deadly thorns. They would scratch along the bodywork of the car, with the screech of chalk on blackboard, and spring into the open window, clutching at your clothing and wildly lacerating your hands and face.

Although the barren landscape seemed to hold very little, it revealed more on acquaintance. I found that the colours subtly alter throughout the day, with a dramatic change in the late afternoon, when the sun begins its journey to meet the horizon. Then, the landscape takes on a rich ochre hue and every dent in the landscape, every house, animal or scrub acacia, is brought into sharp relief with a deep shadow. This is a mellow time, when the herds with their haze of dust make their way home to the village. The villagers call it "cow-dust time". I felt at peace in this empty landscape with its wide horizon - and still do.

Dusty and unrecognisable, my driver, interpreter and I finally got out of the car at a place I was to know very well as Dhordo village. I was met by brilliantly dressed people. The predominating print colours worn by the men were indigo and madder (dark blue and maroon). The men wore turbans and lungies, while the women presented a blaze of colour with their glittering, embroidered tops, floating head coverings and brightly-printed, baggy trousers or voluminous skirts. They wore abundant jewellery in the nose and ear and around the neck and in bracelets from wrist to armpit. I was spellbound and entranced by the exotic beauty presented to my gaze.

The gentle natural colour of the round mud buildings of the village with their pretty thatch, with each house standing on its apron of mud platform, raised to be above the monsoon waters and so protecting the house, formed a perfect backdrop to the brightly clothed women and men. I had chanced upon a story from the Arabian Nights and felt that a tale from Scheherazade would unfold. Indeed, there was a story unfolding: it was the beginning of my story.

My host, Shri Gulbeg himself, came to meet us, and Mr Davi explained that I was a lecturer and had come to study Indian textiles and that my purpose in visiting the village was to see the embroidery in Dhordo village and the different embroideries executed in the various villages in Banni. Gulbeg was very happy to help and kindly invited me to stay with his family. So began my first visit and my lifetime's friendship with this village and its family members. My fears of being welcome to stay were very quickly dispelled, and as you will see I was clearly treated as the honoured unexpected guest, and indeed have always been so.

Now that my guide, Mr Davi, was assured that I would be well-cared for, he set out on his return journey to Bhuj, with instructions to come back for me in five days' time. As for myself, I had

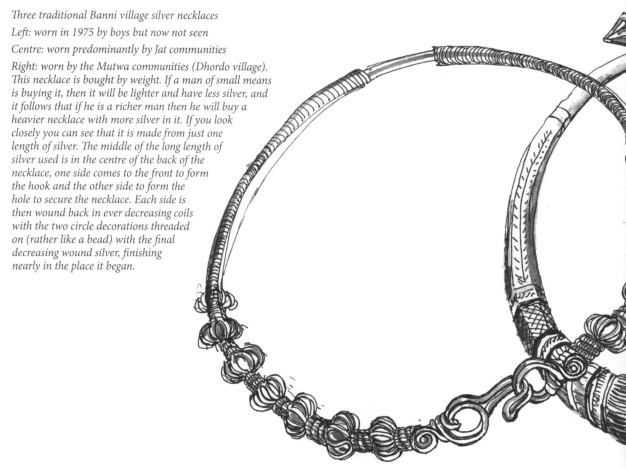

Three traditional Banni village silver necklaces
Left: worn in 1975 by boys but now not seen
Centre: worn predominantly by Jat communities
Right: worn by the Mutwa communities (Dhordo village). This necklace is bought by weight. If a man of small means is buying it, then it will be lighter and have less silver, and it follows that if he is a richer man then he will buy a heavier necklace with more silver in it. If you look closely you can see that it is made from just one length of silver. The middle of the long length of silver used is in the centre of the back of the necklace, one side comes to the front to form the hook and the other side to form the hole to secure the necklace. Each side is then wound back in ever decreasing coils with the two circle decorations threaded on (rather like a bead) with the final decreasing wound silver, finishing nearly in the place it began.

packed a few, essential items of clothing, as well as my sense of adventure and spirit for enjoying whatever unfolded.

Most of my clothes were suitable but, over the following days when I travelled out into Banni, Mrs Gulbeg insisted I use one of the long ordanies to more fully cover my head and upper body as better protection against the dust. (Ordanies are women's head coverings like a big, long scarf, often with an embroidered band where it goes round the head and face, and is worn by the ladies with it flowing down the back from the head.)

The village of Dhordo was entered through the reception building, which, although now extended, is the same building with the same logo "Wel * Come" on the wall. This room acted as a meeting place for officials from Bhuj and for villagers walking across Banni to speak and confer with Mr Gulbeg. As head man to all the villages, he was a very active man, well-respected by both the villagers and the local government. To speak to Mr Gulbeg, villagers may well have walked for two days or more to get to Dhordo. The village extended hospitality to all these people

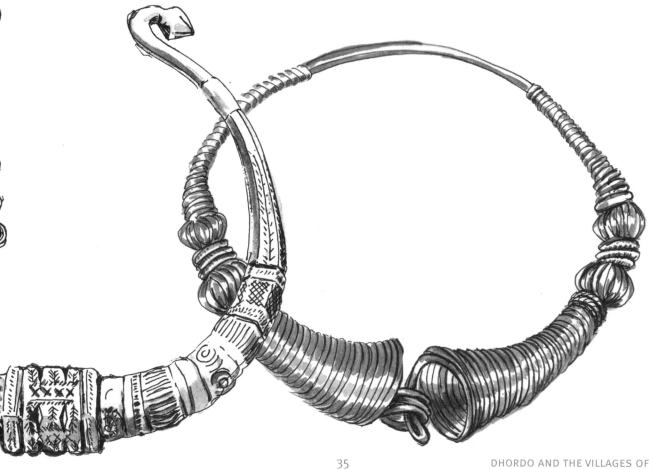

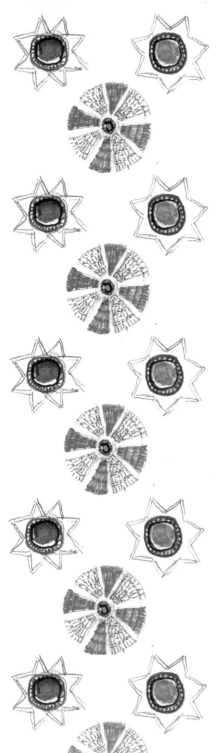

and they were fed and often slept overnight in the reception room before returning to their village. This is mostly the same today, except they will probably come by jeep.

The village houses were then predominantly circular, built with mud walls and with thatched roofs. At no time have they been built to any ordered plan but have been erected cheek-by-jowl as the demand for another house has arisen. I will talk in greater detail about the buildings in the following chapters.

As a guest with the Gulbeg family, I stayed in their large, round house. An evening meal was brought in and served on a metal communal plate. This huge plate was set on the floor in front of all the family members, which comprised Mr Gulbeg and Mrs Gulbeg and their three children. Before eating, Mrs Gulbeg brought a one-spouted brass pot of water with which we perfunctorily washed our hands, as a little water was poured over them into a bowl beneath.

The various dishes served on to the communal platter comprised curried meat, chunks of jaggery (a solid of cane sugar), curd in a separate dish set onto the platter, vegetable curry, roasted chillies and a stack of heavy millet chapatis garnished with ghee. To accompany the meal came a large jug filled with buttermilk, which was poured into steel tumblers.

The meat curry was very highly spiced for me, bringing tears to my eyes; the cooling curd was a lifesaver. But it was a hearty robust meal. In all Indian meals there should be several components. At a simple village level, as in this meal, it comprises protein (meat), carbohydrate (millet chapatis), minerals (vegetables) and some sweetness. Sweet items can be eaten at any time in the meal and are always served at the same time as the other dishes.

Indian meals should always have many different tastes: spicy, with bland curd to offset this, chillies or lime giving sharpness or sourness, and then sweetness as in the jaggery. This is a simplistic outline of the composition of Indian cuisine and in an expert's hands would be extolled to a much greater degree.

We ate with one hand, each dipping into the same dish. I was not very dextrous at this and am still not very accomplished today. After the meal, water was poured over our hands again.

Above: Shisha embroidery with stitched motif found in Mutwa work.

Opposite: on the right is a circular container for grain storage (the grain is poured in the top and let out by removing the stopper in the central motif). Next to it is a cupboard for keeping textiles in. The base relief decoration is embedded with mirrors, the designs closely following the embroidery patterns.

My next uncertainties were to do with bedtime and where the lavatory and bathroom were. It was indicated to me that one took a small water pot and made for the great outside. Luckily for me, it was the seventies, when full, long skirts were the fashion. I just sank down with my skirt billowing out around. The water pot for washing was very hygienic. There was no need for toilet paper, not that there was any in any case, as no toilet paper was then available in India. I found Indians to be very tactile - using their hands (or, rather, different hands) to eat with and to wash themselves. The village was then whistle clean, as were all villages and towns and cities throughout India. There was no plastic at this time, and all other rubbish was bio-degradable.

My next concern was to discover what one did at bedtime. I guessed one just jumped into bed fully clothed. I got that right but did not allow for washing my feet by the same method with the water pot. Shoes were normally not worn in the village but, if worn, never in the house, so feet were washed before bedtime. My bed was brought into the round house. I and Mr Gulbeg slept on charpoys, the traditional rope-strung, wooden-framed beds, while the children and Mrs Gulbeg slept on the floor. We all had beautifully hand-embroidered quilts to put over us.

I also discovered where the bathroom was - through a door in the round house - and I was provided with a bucket and scoop and a pot of hot water to go with the half bucket of cold water that was supplied for me every day from the village well. Pouring water over oneself in a semi-desert area has to be one of the most refreshingly enjoyable experiences, with the sound, and above all the feel, of the poured water over my body.

I remember always wanting to wash my hair, which quickly got stiff with dust. After I had washed it, it almost immediately got dusty again. One learnt to cover the hair as the villagers did. I also learnt to wash my hair with the local clay as shampoo and to rinse it in buttermilk. The result was very good.

I spent five magical days with the family. Gulbeg spoke some English and his daughter, Poppeli, aged sixteen, and son, Ali Akbar, aged fourteen, both knew some words, which was enough. Gulbeg was a wonderful host and over the next few days he drove me out to the most important different communities in his jeep. The jeep is the ship of the Banni semi-desert and Gulbeg as headman had several. The jeep was open-sided and, to help the flow of the dust, the windscreen was opened up. This made the dust flow over us rather than be funnelled into a current which would sweep in at the sides. I put my sunglasses on and wound Mrs Gulbeg's long ordani more securely round my head against the dust. It was fresh and exhilarating to drive over Banni in the jeep.

Visits to Jat, Pathan, and Harijan communities

There are four highly distinctive communities in Banni: my host village Mutwa, Jat, Pathan and Harijan. We made three important visits across Banni to see these last three communities. I will list the other communities and their embroidery later but these are the four most relevant groups. Each has distinct differences in both the work and the garments they embroider and wear. I cannot emphasise enough the abundantly rich experience I gained from all my Banni visits.

The Jat community

The first highlight was when we went across the Rann to see the remote Jat people in Bhritara Mota. The custom was that I first sat with Mr Gulbeg and the elders of the village. We would be served chai, which is definitely India's espresso. I should take time to tell you about chai, as it is the pervasive drink in Kutch. Chai is usually made with boiled milk and water, although very often in Banni there would be no water and it would be made completely with buffaloes' milk, often procured on the spot. The milk is boiled with spices such as ginger in winter and often with cardamom. When boiled, tea and sugar are added and boiled again together. Water from a steel flask is drunk before taking the chai (as indeed one does with espresso). Just as espresso coffee is a small, concentrated drink served in small cups, so chai repeats this, being small in quantity: it is served in very delicately patterned small cups and saucers.

Jat girl wearing the dress of her community at this present time. Formerly in 1975 they wore an ankle-length dress without the trousers.

39

Very often people will share a cup, with one person having the saucer and the tea poured into it from the cup and supped from the rim. I have been in poor villages where they only had saucers. The taking of tea is a great pleasure. It is a sharing ritual and is so fragrant and refreshing that one can exist for the day on tea only. Indeed, we spent the next few days doing just that.

I walked through the village to where a throng of giggling women and children were excitedly awaiting me. We had no common language, but women have a kinship here and are used to the firm bonding between females, and again it was an occasion of great mutual interest. They had never seen a Western woman, and my white skin caused great interest. I got pinched several times, but all in good fun. They brought a charpoy out and spread a patchwork quilt for me to sit on and then spread it with their beautiful embroideries.

The embroidery consists of heavy, solidly-embroidered square fronts for the women's dresses, and squares for oblong bags. What makes their embroidery so heavy is that it could be called 'double work', as there is first a laid thread which is then whipped over. Although this makes the work twice as long to execute, it is stronger and gives it a ridged, raised appearance. The women also make appliquéd quilts, as do all the Banni villages. The Jat, however, are the only Banni community to wear dresses.

I wanted to buy an embroidery, but the Jat are proud people and did not sell their embroidery (although at a later date they allowed me to buy a dress-front to become a part of my sabbatical

Above: a rubbing of the silver hair clip (actual size) worn on the back of the head by Jat women. From the loop in the top of the clip, black threads are tied which go over the head and are tied to the top of the nose ring to support its weight. The nose ring is put on at the time of marriage.

The nose ring also illustrated is drawn to actual size and you can see why it needs to be supported in the manner described above. Note the thickness of the gold hoop which passes through the nose!

Right: a woman from the Jat community.

year's study collection). In the intervening years, when the monsoon has not come and Banni has become more of a desert, the ensuing hardship has caused the Jat to have to sell their work. Which is a sadness in itself.

The Jat are most distinctive in their dress[1] and jewellery. The adults wear either a full-length red or black dress. From infancy girls wear a black dress. The red dress is the bridal dress and is worn until it has become rags, and is then replaced with the black dress. This too is worn until it also falls to pieces, which will take many years, and is then replaced with another black dress.

---

1 *See illustration of dress on page 59*

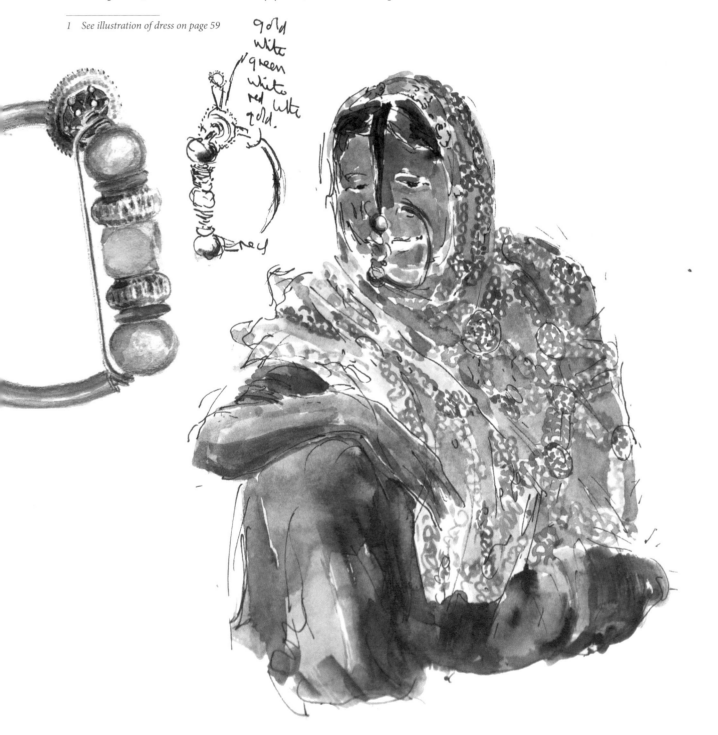

It is said that 500 years ago a pir (holy man) died, and the ladies wore black to mourn him and have never come out of mourning.

Mr Gulbeg made a very memorable remark about the Jat dress. He said, "Lorna, a Jat lady's whole life is lived in her dress. It is a history and diary of her life."

The other most distinctive aspect of the Jat women is the nose ring. This is put on at the time of marriage. It is a half ring of gold measuring some four inches in diameter. This half ring is passed through the nose and, between the two ends of the ring, heavy glass and gold beads are threaded on what could be described as a safety pin which fastens the two open ends of the ring. The nose ring is so heavy that it has to be supported. This is done with black threads which are tied to the ring and passed over the head, to be held in place with a heart-shaped, silver clasp on the hair at the back of the head. This is not seen, as the head is covered with the ordani. The women also wear distinctive earrings and the heavy necklace common in a variety of styles worn in all the Banni villages.

I understood that only if the ladies gave permission should I take a photograph. Then as now, it is a strong Muslim belief that being photographed means having your spirit taken away. This is always a sensitive area and must be respected.

In 1975, the time of this my first visit, many women had never left this village, Bhritara

Azimatbai on the left, the mother of Noori on the right, two women of the Pathan community. Their embroidered tops are richly embroidered and further embellished with both silver and gold work - plus pom poms.

Mota, during their whole lives. It is only recently that more vehicles are driven to the village or owned by a village member. There is still no road to the village.

In 1975, it took eight days on camel-back to get from the village to Bhuj. Shopping was done by the men and this is still the normal practice for all the Banni villages. But, because of this very remoteness, it has held the traditions of dress, jewellery and customs for a longer period, not only in this community but in all the Banni communities.

While crossing Banni, we were lucky enough to come upon a group of Rabbari (whom I have described earlier in their white and black outfits) with their herds of camel. Only the menfolk were with the camels. They were camped and had tied the young camels to the bushes. The females were free to roam but would not go far as they would return to their young to feed them. I was offered camel's milk, which was then all the Rabbari lived on when they took the herds out for many days' grazing in Banni.

To milk the camel, the herdsman makes a crook of his knee, which creates the right height for balancing the pot under the camel's teat. The camel has two teats; while the baby camel takes the milk from one side, the herdsmen takes it from the other.

I recall the hiss of the milk into the pot. Its consistency was thin, not creamy like full cow's milk. It was naturally warm, coming direct from the camel, and tasted salty, with the head of a good Guinness. It was a very interesting experience. The herdsman would also pass the time smoking home-made 'biddies' (or local cigarettes) made out of tobacco rolled in acacia leaves.

43

The other pastime was combing and spinning the camel hair. The herdsmen combed for three colours, light brown, mid brown, and black or dark brown. They then spun the wool by the drop spindle method. (I do not know if this art is still practised; I have not seen it for many years.) On returning home, this thick wool was spun to a finer thread by the womenfolk. It was then plied and intricately plaited or spangled, but not woven, by the women into camel straps and netted bags for the male camel's testicles. The bags are made to stop the animal breeding all the time. The wool is sometimes woven into camel blankets but I never encountered this in Kutch, only in Rajasthan. I have some wonderful straps in my collection with depictions of goats and camels, the ending tassels being four-sided plaits. At another time I saw goat's hair being used and combed for black and white thread.

The Pathan community

The next distinctive community was the Pathan. The community I visited was in the interior of Banni and another day's jeep journey away. The chief difference in their work lies in the heavy use of gold and silver thread. The Pathan's traditional costume is a very long top with a full back, with the baggy trousers of the Mutwa, my host community. The embroidered motifs used are similar to the Mutwa, excepting that the Mutwa is distinguished by the minute size of the stitches and the smallness to which the shisha mirrors are cut before being stitched into the embroideries. No community can match the Mutwa for fineness of work and execution.

The Pathan embroidered tops, while using similar but bigger embroidered motifs, are often enlivened with some gold-work motifs. However, it is when it comes to special celebration tops for a marriage or the birth of a child that their distinctive use of gold and silver thread-work is shown. They use two threads stitched in several designs. It is a surface-laid thread with a matching-coloured, cotton thread couching it down. The continuing laid thread is formed into designs, rather like taking a line for a walk. The lines being sewn next to each other achieve a solid mass. The gold-worked tops present a splendidly solid appearance, which does away with any need for jewellery as it is often formed in heavy scrolls and solid circles of gold round the neck of the top.

Two bands of bold embroidery executed by the Harijan community.

I clearly remember visiting the main oblong room in the small hamlet of Jurawada in 1975. It is a tradition of each village house to place precious items, such as sets of cups and saucers, on the shelf running round the room below the eaves. This shelf also held empty medicine bottles, tapes which were broken, a dead torch and several batteries. There were many more items but it showed just how valuable and how scarce material objects were for these people. For me it had all the beauty of more precious items. Rather like modern art where a single item is chosen, so one's gaze and intellectual thought transform it into a work of beauty.

The Harijan Community

The last outstanding community are the Harijan. These are the lowest caste of Hindu religion, formerly called 'the untouchables'. They have small settlements in many of the Muslim villages of Banni. It should be explained that in a Banni village there is very often not just one community but possibly several different Muslim communities, besides an enclave of Harijan. Birendira, Gorivalie, Hodka and Ludia are four such villages with large communities of Harijan, while in Dhordo there is a small enclave of Harijans.

The coexistence of the Harijan with other communities throughout Banni has come from mutual benefit and need, and are to be found as small communities in each and every Banni village. The Harijans are the caste which will deal with dead animals. No other Hindu caste will do this job. The Banni Muslim communities are all pastoralist and are concerned with raising and selling cows, buffalo, sheep and goats. The Harijan cannot breed cattle. On the contrary, their caste skills are killing animals for meat, the disposal of dead animals, and the tanning of the skins. So an amicable inter-reliance has evolved over the centuries. The Harijan ladies will also clean for the Muslims, and are skilled in the art of mud-work decoration. In 1975, the ladies were executing mud-work building in Dhordo.

The Harijans made at this time many beautiful leather items inlaid with intricately pierced work. In 1975, the pierced work was done with gold and silver lines for precious items such a marriage shoes and horse accoutrements. Work such as this is still executed, but not to the same high degree, the Harijans having now all but lost the fine craft and art of piercing and inlay.

My view of Harijan embroidery work is that I see it as mimicking that of the Banni Muslim communities. The Harijans who have settled here have adopted embroidery alongside their Muslim neighbours and the traces of the adopted designs are easy to recognise once one is conversant with the Muslim originals.

This is not to say that I undervalue their work, quite the contrary. Their work has a flamboyance and robustness of colour and design which brings together many of the patterns in a more intense form. For instance, they have developed and enlarged the small delicate designs of the Mutwa, so making the embroidery into a blaze of concentrated colour. The Harijan have also incorporated many Jat motifs, although leaving out the double stitching of the Jat. This makes the work faster to execute but of a lesser solidarity, as it is only half the work. However, it is again flamboyant. The stitch that is their own original is the even step stitch[1], which looks like counted work but is executed purely by the judgement of the eye. This even step stitch decorated their quilts, and is still in use, though now much adulterated and adopted by other communities.

The Harijans wear their long tops with very full gathered skirts. The ordani head-covering often had (and still has) a heavy, brocaded material band going over the face and hair section. This material is often applied as a border to the hem of the skirt, so making it stand out.

Gorivali is not far from Dhordo, and I remember cycling over the dusty terrain to see it with Ali Akbar. I was struck by the densely colourful garments of the Harijans and the fact that they used rather more literal designs in their work, whereas Muslim designs are all purely abstract. The Harijan had mud-work on one of the house walls which portrayed peacocks in base relief. It was such a spirited rendition.

Mutwa embroidery and shisha mirror

Mutwa, my hosts village, is the fourth most distinctive community which I found in Banni. Its embroidery prides itself on its perfectly executed minuteness of stitch and the smallness of the shisha mirrors embroidered into it. In her book *Sketches from Cutch*, Marianne Postens writing in the 19th Century makes reference to Cutch ladies' dress: she is referring to ladies from the area between Bhuj and Mandvi, South Kutch. But the mirror work equally applies to the Banni villages.

> 'the peculiar fashion of ornamenting the hems of their garments with a phylacterie of little silver bells; and decorating their bodices with little pieces of looking glass, which are sewn in with the embroidery.'

I love the description of wearing little pieces of looking-glass, which, of course, describes a variation of the embroidery we see here in Banni. This looking-glass (called shisha), which all the ladies in Banni use, was in 1975 hand-blown outside Bhuj. Now it comes from elsewhere in Gujarat but is still made in the same way. The mirror glass is hand-blown into large balloons,

---

1   *See illustration page 233*

A women seeing in the doorway of her house.

Boree.

adlatov

goutas

parow.

kuttoree

parow.

dropat

kuttoree

dricken

pucko

kach.

parow

Kach

which, when cooled in the sand, are broken into shards and the pieces sold by weight in Bhuj bazaar. If a lady is from Banni, her husband, who does all the shopping, will buy the glass for her. In 1975 a wife was then in self-imposed purdah and did not leave the village unless in very unusual circumstances. When she did she would pull her ordani down over her face and walk behind her husband. This is still very much the custom today.

As every Banni village lady and girl from the age of six years embroidered every day, there was a high demand for the mirror glass and the making of the globes was thus a thriving trade.

Each of the twelve communities which make up all the Banni Muslim communities, plus the Hindu Harijans, cut the glass with scissors, and the edges are filed to the size and shape of each embroidery's tradition. Thus, the Jats often use triangle shapes, often in excess of one inch, while the Mutwa cut the glass to less than a quarter of an inch. So, when ringed with the buttonholed embroidery, the circumference showing is less than one- eighth of an inch. It is a twinkle rather than a flash. They also use a feather stitch of minute proportion and are well known for using a stitch, known as Gujarati stitch, which is an intricate, surface-laced stitch. We know it as Maltese Cross.

There are set patterns with known names for the motifs. A lady would perhaps feel uncertain as to her artistic skill and would take it to a man or woman who would draw her design onto the fabric for her. The ink was made in the old-fashioned way, called 'lamp black', by holding a saucer over a candle flame. The soot was mixed with a little ghee and then used as a paint.

In 1975 the Mutwa wore both backless tops and fully backed tops. They said a young woman had to wear a full top, as a man's gaze would be on her, although her ordani would cover her back. So, only older women wore the backless top. But this was not always so. The backless top was held in place with two long strings tied in a bow in the middle of the back. Women looked very handsome in them, and the glimpse of the lithesome body and bare back was always a delight. Now the traditional embroidered top is worn only by older women and at weddings, and all with the full back.

Left: Mutwa motifs with the name next to it, by which it is known. Drawn in 1975.

Right: a wooden carved and lacquered spindle for keeping the embroidery threads, like a series of cotton reels. The Harjan community make the pretty lacquered spindles. Painted in 1975.

49

It is interesting to recall that the sari was originally worn without the top, the sari alone wrapping the breasts. When Wellesley became Viceroy, he brought two things to India – Christianity and Western women. The prudishness of the British women combined with Christianity brought about the change in the wearing of the sari.

On this first visit I was shown a pair of ladies' antique silk trousers. They were shaped like a very long bridge, the gap between the two legs being some one and a half yards. The trousers were like pyjamas with a cord round the waist. When this length was pulled up to the waist, it produced with the long top a very graceful effect, the many folds of the trousers pushing through the side opening of the top. Heavy silver anklets were also worn with this.

The tradition in the village in 1975 was that, when the ladies' and girls' work was done, they would spread a quilt on the ground outside their door and sew. Their neighbours, friends and kith and kin would join them and sometimes there was enough time off from household duties to embroider for up to six hours a day. During this time one or other lady would bring a kettle of chai and serve tea to all. It was a friendly, convivial atmosphere, with all the ladies and girls chattering and gossiping and sharing news.

At this time there was little education, and for girls it was only thought necessary that they should learn the Koran. So a girl began to sew for her dowry very early.

To sit with these graceful people and watch them doing this matchless work and creating perfect masterpieces of embroidery was a joy. The time flew, as it does when every day is packed with such rich experiences, and, all too quickly, my car, driver and Mr Davi arrived to take me back to Bhuj.

Lacquered Khole pot (1975). Khol is a black cosmetic which the ladies used to put round their eyes and the eyes of the children.

Chapter 3

The pastoralist way of life

Jat, Pathan, Harijan and Mutwa are the predominant communities known for their distinctive needlework. They, and all the twelve communities which make up the Muslim population of Banni, are also known as Maldheri – breeders of cattle. The villager from Banni wears the name Maldheri with pride, and justly so. His ancestors, and the ancestors of the other Banni communities, came into this tract of grassland and settled it community by community over several centuries. Generation after generation has pursued the breeding of strong, hearty livestock as the sole means of employment. On my first visit, all the villagers were pastoralists. Now, though all the villages will still proudly refer to themselves as Maldheri, the grass is no longer sufficient to support this way of life. Migration has started, other employment is sought and there is much poverty in many villages.

Banni is a tract of unfenced land which runs below the Great Salt Rann, which forms a natural barrier and is now the border between India and Pakistan. When people first settled there, it had abundant grass and wells, as a map shown to me by His Highness, surveyed and drawn by the English in the early part of the 18th Century, illustrates. It has Banni very accurately defined and written over with the text "Banni a tract of grasslands with abundant wells". The map bears the English spelling for the kingdom – Cutch rather than Kutch – and was drawn and shows Banni before the earthquake. The earthquake was of such magnitude it altered irrevocably the geography and terrain and in particular altered the course of the Indus. It took away the fresh delta waters and the rich silt carried with it and instead letting the Arabian seawater seep over the Rann. In the course of time this has in places created a thick layer of white salt.

While the name Maldheri is common to all the Banni villages, each community adopted different husbandry. Some reared sheep and goats and cows, while others reared camels or buffalo. There were different permutations but all were pastoralists.

In Dhordo, their specialisation and husbandry was in breeding cows. Milk was not a commercial product but was produced primarily for the villagers' own domestic consumption. During the monsoon the village could be cut of for several months, but when it was dry and the lorry could reach the village, surplus milk would be collected, but otherwise leftover milk was made into

Royal elephants

ghee (clarified butter). In 1975, the villagers of Dhordo changed from breeding cows to buffaloes, as cows were not thriving so well. It was felt at this time that this was due to their eating the newly planted acacia. The acacia was being heavily planted throughout Banni at this time, which was a Government scheme implemented to hold the topsoil.

When I first came to Banni the area was still an open tract of open grasslands devoid of trees, the acacia having only been introduced a couple of years prior to my visit. It must have been very rich with abundant grass and water to support so many pastorialist communities to roam and settle here. According to verbal history given to me by the separate communities (detailed in Appendix 1), their ancestors have been living here for between four to five hundred years.

That the land was always rich in grass has been shown by the recent important excavations at Dholavira, situated above and to the eastern side of Khavda in the Little Rann and adjacent to the Great Rann. Archaeology dates the excavated city to have been built some five thousand years ago, corresponding to the Indus valley settlements of Mahenjaro. It follows that this Harappan city must have been built where there was abundant water and plentiful land to support such an important settlement. Now, it is stranded in the salt marsh of the Little Rann.

Oral history tells us that Kutch over the centuries has suffered many changes in the landscape, due overall to the terrain being on a fault line, so causing earthquakes of great magnitude to occur throughout its history.

Previous page: a herdsman wearing an old fashioned turban called a rumal and tied in a style now not often seen but typical of 1975.

We have on record two huge earthquakes which happened on precisely the same fault line and strongly mimic each other in their strength and the damage caused to the same townships. The first occurred in 1819, which has been recorded by the British, and the next happened on the 26 January 2001, some 192 years later. The earthquake of 1819 is responsible for taking the river Indus melt-water away from the Rann and allowing the Arabian sea water to enter the Rann in greater proportion. We have an interesting report on this earthquake from Marianne Postans; she was stationed in Bhuj for several years as part of the British Residency. She writes in 1839 as follows:

> *'Much damage was felt all over the province of Cutch. The convulsion was felt all over India but its severity was greater in Cutch than in the neighbouring provinces. One thousand five hundred houses were destroyed in Anjar and about two hundred lives lost. Bhooj, however, appears to have been most severely visited by this calamity; nearly seven thousand houses were destroyed and not fewer than eleven hundred and fifty people buried in the ruins. To increase the confusion, the royal elephants broke from their pickets, and rushed through the city, spreading terror around and causing incalculable mischief, until stopped by the falling houses.*
>
> *During the first great shock, which occupied about two minutes, the town of Bhooj became nearly a heap of ruins; and from East to West, did the angel of destruction sweep over this devoted province: from Wagur to Luckpat on the Indus, all the stones of the villages were levelled with the dust, and all the towns and forts were materially injured.'*

The low browed hill and the fairy blue of the sk

mirrored in the water is something to remember.

On 26 January 2001 an earthquake occurred of the magnitude 7.6 energy of a mega tonne of a 5.3 hydrogen bomb, with 75% destruction of Bhuj and causing 20,085 deaths.

In 1975, on my first visit, the Government initiative for planting the acacia tree in Banni had already commenced, in order to help hold the loosening top soil. The acacia appears not in the form of trees but as large grown bushes or shrubs with branches spreading low on the ground. Now, the shrub is everywhere, but the soil has further loosened and degraded. The acacia has become an invasive nuisance, and so much so that there is a new Government plan which pays for charcoal burners to go into Banni to dig out the acacia trees, cut them up into lengths, make kilns and fire them until they become charcoal. Many villagers have now learnt this craft and kilns can be seen smoking quietly over the Rann. Mostly they are built around the villages and along the roadside where the acacia has become so widespread. The charcoal is called 'black gold' by the local people as it has brought a new and welcome income. The acacia has also been adopted by many potters for firing the kiln as it gives a certain lustre to the fired vessels.

The acacia is, however, useful as fencing. Many branches will be cut off and used to make a barricade or corral for holding animals, or for protecting the village or a dwelling from the deprivations of the animals. This barricade looks like a huge, tangled pile of barbed wire and does much the same job, though rather more pleasantly than barbed wire.

I was brought up in Lincolnshire, where the land is also flat and gives you a large sky. Maybe this is why I instantly responded to this landscape and felt secure in its immensity. The cobalt blue sky contrasts with the opaque, raw umber landscape, interrupted with the soft smudge of the scrub acacia and the houses of the village dwellings as they appear in view.

When Banni was first inhabited some five thousand years ago, one can assume that the people were not solely reliant on the monsoon, as they are now. The monsoon is particularly fickle with regards to any precipitation in Kutch. There are two arms of the monsoon entering India approximately on the first of June from the bottom tip of India. The left branch follows up the left coast through Goa and Bombay before entering Gujarat as it blows in from the Arabian Sea. The other arm comes up and across The Bay Of Bengal and brings the monsoon in on the right side, travelling up to the top of India and then rounding and travelling down to Gujarat, where they meet and cause precipitation. But by the time they reach Gujarat both arms may have been exhausted. Kutch is known for its lack of monsoon, and in particular Banni.

Previous page: an exceptional picture of water on Banni. I have never seen such abundant water as I have painted here.

Opposite: Jat adult woman's dress. In 1975 it was made with twenty yards of glazed cotton known as American cloth. At the sides, the yardage is contained by a great number of cartoon pleats (which are edge on pleats) which make a solid rigid block of fabric; thus when the woman is walking it gives great movement to the dress.

58

Mutwa community – one of a special pair of marriage earrings worn looped over the top of the ear, worn and drawn in 1975. Not worn now.

Bamba community

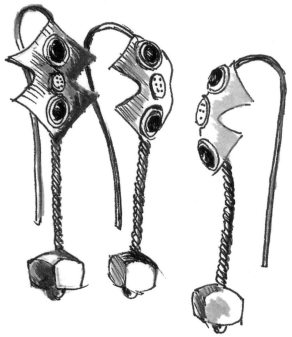

Different communities' earrings. Earrings in 1975 were in sets of up to nine for each ear. The earrings starting at the top of the ear and going right around the ear plus a central stud in the middle of the ear. Over the years this has changed to six then four and now very often not at all. All the earrings are drawn to actual size.

This reliance on the vagaries of the monsoon has gradually come about due to the Indus waters not flowing onto the Rann. The melt-water carried with it rich deposits of topsoil, containing many minerals from the Delta waters, which it deposited on Banni, giving it its abundant grass. Then, with the earthquake of 1819, the course of the Delta waters was changed, and instead of fresh Delta waters carried down from the Himalayas, the Arabian Sea has made an annual inundation and the saline water has distributed layers of salt onto the Rann, souring the once fertile land.

When I first visited, there had been seven years when the monsoon had not come, or else there had been a very low rainfall. Because of the lack of water, the drought had caused the grass to die and the roots which help to hold the soil were coming free, leaving the topsoil to become a moving layer of dust. However, I know that on my first visit Banni was still yielding long grass in the interior, as I saw men bringing in long swathes of grass balanced on their heads for thatching their houses. No houses were tiled at this time, whereas now it is hard to find a thatched house.

Today the scene has greatly worsened. The river, which also emptied into the Rann and so contributed to the irrigation of the grasslands, has now been captured as a reservoir outside Bhuj. Banni was originally watered from three sources: the river emptying its waters into the Rann; the monsoon which was variable; and the primary abundant source, the tributaries of the Indus. Before the huge earthquake of 1819, the melt-water flowing into the eastern sector of the Rann and seeping over the Rann was so abundant that rice crops could be grown on it. The seismic disturbances stopped the melt-water and instead drew in the salt water of the Arabian Sea. Each year, this seepage of seawater onto the Rann has distributed a fine layer of salt, which has now built up into a thick crust. The salt seepage from this has now entered the water table and is making many village wells saline, with several villages having been abandoned.

Standing on the Rann, prisms of light make your eyes blink and half-close against its searing white intensity. Salt crystals caught in the midday sun act in the same reflecting way as frozen crystals of snow, but, instead of snow, one is crunching a thick layer of salt underfoot with a tropical sun overhead. It has a quality all its own, the curved expanse of the cobalt blue sky leaping and reaching to touch a far horizon over a flat, endless plain of white. This landscape, created over a century ago, looks disconcertingly out of place.

Because of the saline water, new and deeper wells have had to be dug, again lowering the water table. On my original visit, well water was abstracted from a well to the right side of Dhordo. Over the years, this well was dug deeper and deeper, with lengths of bamboo supporting the sides. Water was hauled out in a buffalo skin and distributed into a trough for the animals to drink and for the ladies to fill their water vessels. There was also a tank which held monsoon water. A tank not only fills with water but also water seeps directly below the surface of the well and is stored, so when to all appearances the tanks is dry it will still yield

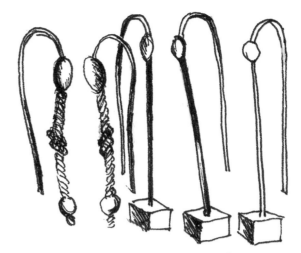

Megwal and Ahir communities outside Banni drawn in 1975

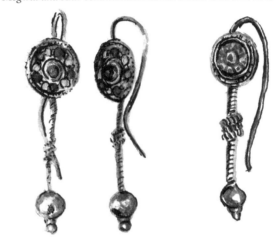

Mutwa community

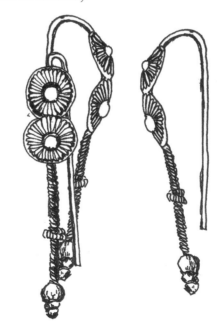

61

Raisiputra, Haliputra and Mutwa communities drawn in 1975.

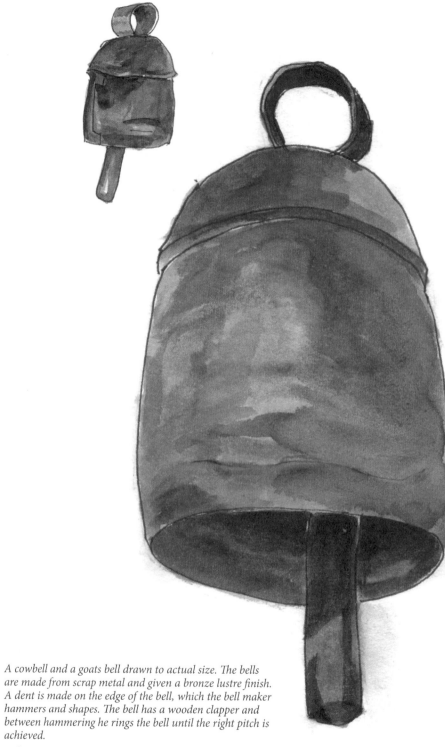

A cowbell and a goats bell drawn to actual size. The bells
are made from scrap metal and given a bronze lustre finish.
A dent is made on the edge of the bell, which the bell maker
hammers and shapes. The bell has a wooden clapper and
between hammering he rings the bell until the right pitch is
achieved.

Left: a piece of gold work embroidery in a traditional design.

water. A bore is made in the middle of the tank and a pump placed over it. The water is then pumped to the surface.

In 1975, the traditional lifestyle of the Mutwa was still able to be sustained. Now, this is not the case. The tradition then was that, after the monsoon, the herd grazed round the village when the grass was fresh and long. When this was eaten, the herds were taken into Banni for several days at a time, each time the herdsman taking them further and further into Banni.

This practice was common to all villages, but each community developed its own practice. The Jat, for instance, went on what they called 'pukko.' The whole village, with the exception in the main of the old people, would travel out. They would take temporary tents made of finely woven cane mats, which would be propped up to make the camps. The villagers would take the herds of buffalo and sheep and roam the grasslands, going right into the interior.

I remember, while on one visit in 1986, travelling over Banni and coming across a group of migrating Jat. A baby had just been born and it was brought out for me to see and as they viewed my unexpected visit as auspicious they brought it out for my blessing. Great was my surprise when I was given a swaddled baby to hold; I had never seen swaddling before. The baby had a board down its back and was tightly cross-bandaged rigidly strapping the length of its little body. I have never seen this practice since.

It was a beautiful group of Jat. Many of the men had bright red hennaed hair, the belief being that henna keeps the head cool. They carried long poles for herding. The children were all wearing perfectly embroidered, clean dresses, as were the women. They brought out their embroidery all carefully wrapped, as was the custom in all the communities. The embroidery work was rolled, with only the portion waiting to be embroidered showing. This keeps the work perfectly clean.

At the time of my first visit, as I have said, ghee was commonly made in Dhordo and in all the Banni villages. It formed a crucial part of their diet, and was used extensively in cooking. Like a preserve it could be stored for long periods. Ghee was especially made during the monsoon period, when any surplus milk could not be kept as there was no refrigeration, and the milk lorry which came at intervals through the week could not reach the village, which could be cut off for months. Now that there is a road to Dhordo, there is a daily milk collection from the string of villages which border the road. Surplus ghee would have been sold at local markets, and gave ready money for the women to purchase items when pedlars came to the village.

Dairying was, however, never the real trade. Maldheri, as I have said, are known for being breeders of animals, for meat rather than dairying. (Kutch Rabbari are the Hindu group whose husbandry is the production of milk.) Rabbari do not live in Banni but have wandering rights over the terrain. The road to the village was constructed in the 1980's, not to improve the villagers' communications but for the defence of the country, should there be a war with Pakistan.

As has been noted, the village houses throughout Banni were then predominantly circular, built with mud walls and with thatched roofs. The houses were made in the old way of wattle and daub. To make the walls, a trench was dug and lengths of thin branches were then buried in the trench and interlaced within the basic structure. Soil was mixed with buffalo or cow dung with water added, the fibres from the dung binding the soil, so making it strong. The walls were made by building up the layers of mud until a thick, robust wall was achieved. Four apertures were commonly made at the opposite points, three as windows with the fourth being the doorway. Window openings were barred by the branches passing through. If a person was better off, then glazed windows were put in with shutters. The shutters and doors would often have surface carvings on them.

The roofs being thatched let the smoke from the cooking fires filter through. This also acted as ventilation, allowing the passage of air to filter and keeping the interior cool. The houses were also cool because of the thick mud wall. With the modern adoption of tiled roofs, the cooking is now often done outdoors or in a separate kitchen, and with the tiles the houses are hotter than before.

The grass thatch was pegged down with ropes made of the grass. At the eaves a plait was made with the end of the roof straw, forming a continual line going round the house. The houses were built on a raised platform of mud in order to stand above the monsoon waters. The platform would be continually refreshed with a new layer of mud spread by hand upon it. This would be done as frequently as once a week. It presented a tactile quality, as the surface held the sweeping fan movements of the hands and fingers which smoothed it, as did the house walls. The house walls bear hand marks and ridges in the same way as a pot from a potter's wheel. Against this gentle, sepia-coloured village of thatched mud buildings, the men, women and children in their bright clothes made a pretty picture.

The hairstyle of the women and children at the time of my first visit was very distinctive. The hair was turned under from the front parting and plaited round the head to the back, making it look like a fitted, black cap. It always seemed to me that the hairstyle reiterated and mimicked the plaited house thatch![1]

In the young children's earlobes the broken-off ends of the thorn from the acacia tree could be found. The thorn was used to pierce the ears and was then broken off and left until the hole was healed. Then, pieces of embroidery thread would be put through and, at a later stage, the first rings.

---

1   See the images of the Harijan girl on the title page of chapter 15 and the Appendix page which is a Jat girl. Both these images show the hairstyle described here.

In Dhordo and in all Banni villages at that time, nine rings were worn right round the ears. When a girl became a teenager, the first rings would be replaced with four heavy earrings at the top of the ear in the style worn in the Banni village. The earrings were so heavy the ear would bend over. Following this were five rings, making nine rings as worn in 1975. The earrings would be of silver but, if the family were rich enough, they would be in gold. Girls also wore a piece of jewellery through the central wall of the nose, shaped like a decorative lock. I recently saw this item of jewellery being worn by girls and women on my visit in 2009, when I was lucky enough to go to several weddings. Although now not worn every day, this nose jewellery (see page 156) had been brought out for this special occasion.

The useful two-inch thorn was also employed by me as a pin to secure the embroideries to the mud walls of the houses when I wanted to draw the designs or photograph them. I was also told the thorn was so strong it would play a twelve-inch record. I never witnessed it but, as the thorn would pierce right through a strongly soled shoe, I give credibility to this.

Because of the Banni's isolation and lack of communication with the outside world, I was privileged to witness their unadulterated, distinctive traditions of dress and customs. While crossing Banni, I also saw, on many occasions, the herdsmen from the different communities in their traditional dress with their herds of buffalo, cows, sheep, goats and camels. The herdsmen had faces of great beauty. They had a dignity and nobility of stance born from being alone for many days in the quietness of the Rann. There was simplicity to their lives. They did not deal with the ordinary commerce of the day, all money matters being left in the hands of their womenfolk. Indeed, in the dress top of the Ahir community, the money purse is part of the bodice design, with the pocket for the money placed just under the bosom.

The dark, unsmiling, earring-ed faces of the herdsmen, framed by their turbans, look with personal strength from all my photos of this time.

The quietness of the Rann, with only the call of an eagle or the passing of a fox or a gazelle, is a rich image to recall: and then by contrast the coming across herds of animals with their accompanying music. The animals made up an orchestra by their movements, the music coming from the bells hung round their necks, from light short tinkling staccato notes to deep sonorous booming notes, depending if they were a goat with a small fast moving bell or the lead bull cow or buffalo with a larger bell adding slower longer deep resonate notes to the pastoral scene. Accompanied by their shepherd striding along with his long stick across his shoulders was a scene never to be forgotten.

A herdsman wearing his Ajrakh as a lungi.

Wandering Rabbané

Chapter 4

India then and now

I have so many memories, full of the exuberance and potent flavour of India. The wife of the poet John Betjeman, Lady Chetwode, who lived for many years in India, often remarked that the country was "electric with God". While agreeing with that statement, "electric" for me describes the intense energy of India and the ever changing panorama of life being lived in the raw, right in front of you. The following is a selection of images that are pertinent to my family.

Small children travelling to and from school in a cycle rickshaw, at least eight giggling children sitting on every part of it, their many satchels hanging onto the framework, the rickshaw wallah pushing it slowly on its way. A crocodile of neatly uniformed girls with their black plaited hair in shiny ribbons. Traffic coming the wrong way down the street towards us. Motor rickshaws with festoons of fresh flowers decorating the windscreens, with the pungent joss stick burning below the image of Ganeshe in the centre of the driver's dashboard. Rides in a rickshaw with flashing blades sticking out from the back wheels and rotating like those of the evil charioteer in the film Ben Hur. The startling surprise of a raging hot chilli in your mouth, against a quite different anticipation. Brilliant red jelly-like jam, with an unidentifiable taste, nicknamed by us as "radioactive jam", surely has never been near a fruit-tree, the only jam available in India. Then, as now, the proverbial cow wandering the streets, marauding the vegetable stalls for an odd treat or eating cardboard from a pile of rubbish.

Poona - now spelt Pune - was chosen as the base for my sabbatical year because of its good climate in the Maharashtran western Ghats and its two excellent public schools, Bishops for my two boys and St Mary's for my daughter. We stayed with a doctor and his family until I found a flat. Although impersonal and modern, it was redeemed by being situated within walking distance of the schools, the main shopping street in Poona, and the bazaar.

The youngest of my three children, Tress, was seven years old in 1975. His most salient memory of India at that time was that it was grimy and poor. My family moved from living in a spacious Georgian house with many comforts and accoutrements to a culture where there were virtually no toys, and food was an unfamiliar and often disagreeable experience. Furthermore, school discipline and teaching were similar to what my mother or I had undergone in our school days: the teacher would crack the back of your hand with the ruler, things such as tables were learnt by rote, and spelling tests were frequent.

Each day India presented us with sharp and stark contrasts. It could be an emaciated, threadbare beggar, with his outstretched hand, while on the opposite side of the road a gay and happy procession of people were singing and dancing in a marriage procession. We in the West have contrasts of circumstances but not involving such a wide spectrum or such a wide gulf in fortunes, and not affecting so many people. At the time of Partition the population of India totalled three million. Now there are three million people below the poverty line.

I quickly learnt to carry small change so as to be able to give a few rupees to the beggars, who each had their own place to beg from. We all feared the beggar woman with a snake who was always on the corner of the high street. This woman seemed to lie in wait for us and would brandish the snake's spitting head within a hair's breadth of our faces before giving chase. Any thought of giving her money, was wiped out by our urgent need to escape.

The children all enjoyed the Indian bicycles which they borrowed from time to time. The Indian bicycle has a large bell which resonates with a very loud warning ring. Now the bicycle in India has been replaced by an even greater number of motor bikes, which crowd and choke the roads and are often over-burdened with passengers. You will see three or four people on one bike: typically Dad driving with a child behind and then the mother precariously and disconcertingly holding a baby and sitting side-saddle, with her scarf flying.

Most of the time, motorbike riders do not wear helmets, although this is gradually changing. Riders now often wear masks against pollution, and some lady riders are to be seen swathed and muffled up in scarves and thus totally unrecognisable. I am told that this is not only a protection against pollution but in the emerging modern India she may be riding to an illicit assignation and so wish to remain a mystery of disguise.

Also striking was the ever-changing kaleidoscope of images seen on the street. One would have thought a Bollywood film was in the making, right there in front of you. But no, it was just everyday India. This bombardment of stimuli, so hard to retreat from, can give you the feeling of being besieged. One learns in time to sort out this visual chaos, but first impressions are disorientating.

India is excellent at making one live in the present. The now of today is all important. On the wayside shrines, or on the household shrine, garlands of fresh flowers are placed daily. We in the West would put flowers in a vase of water so that they would be there for the next few days. But in India it is the best and freshest for each new day. The reality is the present. There is no insurance policy for tomorrow: today is all-important.

In 1975, when the connections and communications were so much more uncertain, one got used to patiently waiting, and very used to hearing the comment "Oh, we are on Indian time". Being

Plying thread, a weaver wearing a hat commonly worn in 1975.

on Indian time meant one often waited one or two hours for a person, but one knew they were coming. There was an empathy and underlying trust between people which nowadays we do not have. Did the delays matter? I don't think so. In fact, it had a benefit: one sat and observed India. A very worthwhile pursuit and of particular value in India.

Frequent celebrations sprinkled the calendar and I think they helped to divert the poor people from their poverty and, in many cases, the hopelessness of improving their lot. The many celebrations during our stay would be announced with fire crackers. These were in a bunch or a tied-up bundle and when lit would ricochet and career down the street, giving off bang after bang, scaring the life out of everyone. Indians loved the fright it gave and would laugh like naughty children when they saw your alarmed response. This enjoyment is still evident today.

One of the most celebrated street festivals, particularly in Mahrashtra (where we were), is the festival of Ganeshe, the elephant god. Garishly coloured plaster models of all sizes, from small

ones of six inches to large models of two or three feet, are displayed and sold for a few rupees at every wayside bazaar. The model makers are in full employment from one year's end to another. Ganeshe is a god who is revered by many people as he is deemed auspicious to any business enterprise. At the time of his festival, symbols of the trade one is employed in are placed on the household shrine; for example, for an accountant his accountancy book with some money may be used. The god is called upon in a very practical manner to make the business or enterprise prosper.

Maharashtra in particular celebrates this festival, and the children and I very much enjoyed it. Many larger-than-life-sized effigies were trundled through the streets, with loud bands playing, fire crackers banging and people dancing. India's sacred cows were part of the parade, with their long curved horns painted a festive colour and decked out with embroidered covers, the hump of the cow being accommodated for in the design. I remember that, if the owner did not have

The delicately tinted cows with their pink ears.

embroidered or decorated cow covers, the cow's hide was painted in bright patterns from head to toe.

At the end of the festival, the big idols were taken to the river, and after intonations by the brahmins they were ceremoniously dumped into the river and so disappeared from view.

Monsoons are memorable to the children because of the black rubber shoes they had to wear, rather like cut-off wellingtons, which always filled with water and squelched with every step. In the monsoon the children took the school bus, and had to remember to take their umbrellas, as the bus was old and the umbrellas were needed to stop getting wet through the leaking roof. The rain also brought out the cockroaches in great numbers - which we all hated. They turned up in your bed or in your clothes, so everything had to be inspected before getting dressed.

Our household in our modern, impersonal flat in Poona included Ganga. Ganga was a young girl who was my maid. She came every day and would walk the children to school or to catch the school bus if it was raining. She would also take the children their lunch and, if I was out, collect them from school and make them snacks.

One day Ganga, who was only thirteen, invited us all back to her home, a small square edifice measuring seven feet by seven feet, made of sheets of corrugated iron with a roof of the same material. The floor was earth, beaten down with the passage of feet. There was nothing in it except a few rolls of bedding and a few essential vessels. It did not even have the quality

Wankaneer Palace where we spent Christmas.

Camel parade Rajasthan

of a shed. I remember the monsoon rain dripping onto the floor from one of the rivulets in the roof. We sat on a blanket on the floor while Ganga sent out for Marie biscuits, a luxury bought specially for us at five rupees a packet. While she was so proud to have us Westerners for tea with her family, we were humbled.

The schools were adjacent to each other. The children knew I would let them stay as boarders when I went on study tours. While the boys hated the idea, my daughter could not wait to be a boarder. The day came when I was departing for my first three-week tour to go first to Ahmedabad and then down to Bhuj. I saw the children to school with their suitcases and gave Ganga instructions to go to both the boys' and girls' schools to collect their washing and return the laundry on a two-day basis.

I returned from my three-week visit to find the happiness of the children reversed. The boys who had dreaded it loved being boarders, and my daughter was in tears. I think she found the nuns a little remote and had missed us all greatly. However, the appearance of my boys shocked me. Both of them had abundant heads of hair, reflecting the Western styles of the time. I came back to two boys shorn of their lovely locks and down to a very brutal short back and sides. I was told this was due to an outbreak of nits.

Nits were of pandemic proportions in India. It was an everyday sight to see ladies picking nits out of each-other's and children's hair. During my stay I also got nits. I found it very satisfying to have a friend go though my long hair with a fine comb and pick my nits out. I would liken it to a therapeutic head-massage.

Because visiting Kutch had been such a worthwhile and rich experience for me, I decided to take the children on holiday there for the Christmas and New Year break.

The great steam trains made for broad gauge tracks were exciting for the children to travel on. Vendors and entertainers would come through the carriages. Eunuchs were a great surprise with their comely looks, over-made-up faces and garish dress. In Indian culture at this time they were thought to be propitious at weddings and at births, when they would be called upon to dance. This culture, a part of the Hindu belief system for many centuries, has now all but disappeared. I last saw a group of eunuchs at a fair held for the wrestling I attended (described in chapter six). They were going round propositioning, flirting, and asking for alms. They are very audacious but not without their overplayed charms.

We caught the train down to Bhuj, where Prasad, the district development officer, arranged for us to stay in a Government guest house. It had the added charm for the children in that the local goat had just had two kids, which delighted in jumping all over our beds and furniture.

We stayed a few days in Bhuj before catching a local bus, a real bone-shaker, and arrived some three hours later at Birendira, where we bought the local sweet and waited to be collected by jeep by our host, Mr Gulbeg.

This time we stayed in the reception building, which doubles up as guest house for the unexpected visitor, at the front of the village. It was an advantageous place, as we could observe the various village people coming from far and wide to see Mr Gulbeg. Often we would have two or more people staying overnight in beds alongside ours. The children were a novelty to the village children and were taken off here and there to play. Bicycles were borrowed and on one day we rode with an escort over Banni to the nearby village of Gorivelli. The children, as was I, were told not to go out alone, as we could so easily get lost in the featureless sameness that is Banni.

What is worn is also markedly changed. Now, most men wear western clothes, the big Ajrakh lungi being abandoned for the trousers, except on specific occasions. The Ajrakh turban, particular to the Mutwa community, is not often seen. However, at marriage celebrations it will be worn by some men and is still the preferred head gear of the groom.

Young women and girls have all deserted the traditional attire and now wear dresses with the ordani head covering. The arm bands going up the length of the arm are never seen, and similarly absent are the nine earrings always worn by both girls and women in 1975. Earring holes are still put in the young girls' ears, but only one or two holes in each ear. The traditional heavy silver necklace has also gone and, again, is now worn only by the older women. Over the next few years the remnants of the dress code refined over the centuries will have entirely disappeared.

Last but not least, is the traditional occupation of the Mutwa. In 1975 the Mutwa had vast herds and the grass was good by comparison with the present-day. At the time of my first visit, Mr Gulbeg had five hundred buffalo and cows. The cattle were raised for breeding with a few cows just kept for the household needs. The animals would be sold to communities such as

Pathan community mother and daughter
in their village Zarawda

the Rabbarie who made their living by producing and selling milk. Now, the headman has just five buffaloes, that are milked. This huge change is reflected throughout the village. Different occupations have had to be sought, with nearly all of the men working at the chemical factory built in the 1980's next to the Rann, some seven kilometres from the village.

On this visit in 1975 I remember that the children were given village clothes to wear and they blended in pretty well in spite of their white skin and different speech. Thomasin, my daughter, was the most dazzling as she was decked out in jewellery as well as the embroidered top and baggy pants. I still have the photos from this visit, as do Mr Gulbeg's family. It was an enriching visit that none of us has forgotten. Both my daughter and my youngest son have been back several times to visit the village.

On my first visit I travelled back to Ahmedabad with Prasad, who had Government work to attend to. On the way we stayed overnight with his friend at Wankaneer Palace. Again, we were the unexpected guests. The phone was out of order, we just turned up in the formal, curtained Government ambassador's car with its covered pennant on the bonnet. We were well received by the Raj Kumar (crown prince), Digvijay Sinh, who is now the Maharajah. His father, who was a ruling Maharajah at the time of Partition, was a very well informed man

and spoke of his happy schooldays in the UK. He was a Cambridge man, as was his son. I was invited to stay, and so began my friendship with this family. I owe many friendships to Digvijay's letters of introduction. I have already mentioned my friends in Ahmedabad, where my children and I stayed on our way down to Bhuj. It was fascinating to talk to His Highness. He had come to the throne just prior to the time of Partition, which was a time of great turbulence. Opposite the Palace was the former Residency, and in the Palace he had many framed photos, some of the English residents, some out hunting and others in groups. Wankaneer was an important kingdom, and the Maharajah had the power of sentencing any of his subjects to death. At the time His Highness took the throne, the palace had a hundred servants to run it; now there is just a handful of retainers.

Some years ago, I caught by chance an old film on BBC of a palace wedding. It was of His Highness's wedding in Wankaneer in the 1930's. It showed a very fine parade round Wankaneer with bedecked elephants and bullocks drawing the bridal cart. The special marriage carriage was covered with a beautiful embroidery. This same vehicle is now permanently on display in the palace.

Every Sunday until he died, His Highness would take a car and travel round the borders of his former Kingdom. He believed it to be a marvellous accomplishment that the unity of India had been achieved with every kingdom and state being given up voluntarily without any fighting or loss of life.

My children and I were invited for Christmas, and we took the same route that I had previously done. It is such a good contrast to stay first in the village and then in the Palace. (And that is why this book embraces both.)

Dhordo village lies within the kingdom and the one is closely knit with the other. "Bapu" is how the people in the kingdom address their Maharao or Maharajah. It means "father". This is the respected relationship of the ruler to his people. Above all, what has come over repeatedly is the availability of the Maharajah to his people. He was very approachable: people came for his advice and were given an audience. This is so now even as it was in 1975 and as it was when the Maharajahs were the rulers. I know several royal households whose fathers were previous rulers and the present title holder's advice is still sought by their former subjects. India is a huge country and people like the personal closeness and touch that the ruler offers. The state seems often too remote and impersonal, whereas the ruler is the honoured, respected and informed Bapu/father.

Chariot, each wheel individually suspended. There is no continuous axle. In 1975 at the time of my visit to Wankaneer Palace with the children the Maharani told me how she was taken to her marriage in this Chariot. It was covered with embroideries and pulled by six buffalo adorned with embroidered coverings. The royal family in Kutch also used a similar chariot and one is in the Aina Mahal Museum.

Rabbari women wearing
huge ivory bangles.

On arrival at the palace we brought a chicken with us and presented it to the servant. We were accommodated in the residency block, where each room had the name of a previous state. We were in Bikaner and Dungapur. The palace architecture was imposingly Victorian Gothic and our furniture was Victorian with Twyford's sanitary ware. We each of us had a single brass four-poster bed protected by mosquito nets.

We repaired to the guest dining room to find that our offering of a Christmas chicken had been skinned and curried bright red. It was not the English Christmas dinner we had been expecting. But it was good.

Afterwards, we went over to sit with the royal family. The palace has a huge reception room which is full of photos of Indian royal families and of our own royal family. They were great hunters: stuffed animals rear out from all the walls, and there were tiger skins on the floor with the heads still attached to the stretched skin. My youngest son was not used to sitting formally and making polite conversation - after all he was only seven. We suddenly heard a great roaring and turned to see him having a wonderful tussle with the tiger, with his hand swallowed by the tiger's mouth, obviously enjoying a life-threatening adventure. When I visit now, seeing the tiger again brings a laugh and a sigh of happy remembrance from me.

Snake charmer

Chapter 5

The daily round

I am staying in Sifyer's pretty round house, which she and her husband built at the time of their marriage. The two shallow-carved doors to the house are open and, as I sit drawing, a goat strays in. A little later, two kids come gambolling in to play, and are shooed outside. While I paint designs, children silently peer round the door watching me.

I had forgotten just how wonderful life in Dhordo is: the quiet pace of the day and the grace of the people as they go about their daily round. I have not stayed for a long period of time since I was here in the eighties and, before that, during my first visit in 1975. I am appreciating once again these people and their lifestyles.

Living in Sifyer's fairy-tale house makes me feel rather like Alice in Wonderland. The house with its conical roof is an example of the Mutwa's traditional house, using present-day materials. Measuring about sixteen feet across, it has a tiled roof rather than thatched, and its round wall is pierced by three windows and a door.

Between the two windows opposite the door is a formal arrangement of household items, similar to that in nearly every village house. These items are set on a shallow, raised platform. Taking pride of place in the centre is a beautiful Mutwa embroidered quilt, which covers a neatly-folded, wall-high pile of more quilts. To each side are stacked flower-painted tin trunks, which contain dowry articles and stored embroideries, and next to these rise columns of steel and brass water pots. Completing the arrangement on the platform is a strong, lockable tin cupboard, found in most houses, used for securing valuable items such as jewellery.

The furniture comprises a bed, spread with a patchwork quilt, and tables and chairs, with a carpet on the floor. Running round the top of the room is a shallow, mud-built shelf, crowded with proudly-collected china, glass, and plates. The shelf is faced and decorated with base-relief, patterned mud-work, inset with small circles of mirrors, the designs imitating the motifs in Mutwa embroidery. The same decoration has been carried out round the door, windows, mirror and the china cupboard built into the house wall.

When triggered by the movement of a person or of the fan in the room, this delicate tracery of shisha mirror-work springs to life and becomes a moving, reflecting, kaleidoscope of abstract patterns. Added to this are the shapes on the floor made by the sun passing through the coloured window glass. The mirrors and the glass combine to give the room continuous life and energy.

Over the years, I have been aware of a need to help the women make extra rupees, and so I have created a modest self-help scheme for two villages. The communities involved are the Mutwa and Pathan. I have taken embroidery motifs from traditional garments and set them on mushru fabric, which is the traditional fabric for both villages. Mushru fabric is historically a material specially designed for Muslim men and women to wear. Muslims are not supposed to wear silk next to their skin, so the weavers designed a cloth for them which has cotton on the back and silk on the front. This was originally dyed in natural dyes. Now, synthetic colours are used and the silk has been replaced with synthetic yarn. But it is still a very lovely fabric.

In 1975, mushru was commonly used in embroideries and garments, but gradually, over the years, the weavers moved away from the area, particularly after the earthquake of 2001. This fabric is no longer in common use, but a cheap printed version is still widely used. I therefore buy the material from mushru weavers who live in the north of Gujarat at Pathan - this is not to be confused with the Banni Pathan community. The Pathan where the Mushru weavers live and work was formerly the capital city of the state of Pathan, which was a separate kingdom before Partition.

The embroideries I commissioned for the self-help scheme are made to fit into mounts for cards which I designed and had made in Jaipur. The output of embroidery had previously lagged due to a lack of the mushru fabric, and part of the reason for my stay was to oversee this project, and improve production.

Preceding page: a typical house in Dhordo with the stack of quilts and piled decorated tin suitcases used for storage.

Opposite: interior of Sifyers house, note the display on the shelf running round the top of the house. Shelf and walls decorated in fine mud work.

Interior of a Harijan house. This house is circa 1975 and shows a stronger patterning of the mud-work than the Mutwa on the preceding page. Within the decoration you can see the image of the blouse worn by the ladies at this time. The view through the window shows how the Harijans decorate the exterior of their houses.

Alladin, Sifyer and I spent many enjoyable hours tracing the designs and then punching the designs onto plastic sheets with a pin: these designs were then punched onto the mushru fabrics. Skeins were made from the many hanks of different-coloured threads, each village being given a wide selection of colours. The range of colours is the same as those the women themselves use in their own embroidery.

There are now numerous embroidery outlets creating work in the villages, but both the colour combinations and designs are often foreign to the Mutwa and Pathan's traditional work. I have paid great attention in the commercial work I am promoting, so that it does not deviate from the traditional work and break the fragile thread of what has been orally learned. Each woman chooses her own colours and the designs she knows well.

The Pathan village

Finally, our work was ready to be given to the Pathan village of Jurawada, and Alladin and I set off the next morning at ten o'clock. After leaving the tarmacked road, we lost our way several times while crossing Banni on our way to this remote hamlet. One learns great respect for the local villager, who recognises every tree and track on the journey to his village.

We drew up beside a quietly smoking charcoal kiln, its thin smoke rising in the still air. I took a picture of Alladin beside it. He made a compelling image, with his scarf tied round his head in the tradition of the Mutwa.

A striking young man, who was the headman, came to meet us. Dressed in a faded, dusty-black salwar khamez, with his very black skin tone and matt thick black hair stiff with dust, he was a colour co-ordinated vision, relieved by the slash of the vivid pink scarf round his neck. A rope circled his waist, with the long knotted ends being passed through his hands in the manner of a monk telling his rosary. Framed by the dun-coloured semi-desert and the bhunga houses of his village behind him, a more picturesque man would be hard to find.

Above: traditional mushru fabric used in Mutwa embroidery 1975 now not often used.

Opposite: Sifyer tracing embroidery designs onto cloth.

From the distance of the village hamlet, first one woman saw and recognised me, and then another. As word went round, the women began to come out of their houses to greet me with much chattering and smiles. They presented a nostalgic picture for me, as they were all dressed much the same as in 1975. Because this small village is not served by a sealed road, or indeed by any road, and lies within the Banni tract of land, its very isolation has preserved this hidden treasure. Just as the dress is still in its traditional form, so are the dwellings, which due to the village's poverty continue to be constructed in wattle and daub.

The women hugged and kissed me and seized my hand with their rasping grip. I always wonder how they execute such fine embroidery when their hands are so hard and calloused by the work they do. I then shook hands with all the men and gave boiled sweets to the children, but as the grownups also liked the sweets they got them too.

Quietly smoking charcoal kiln

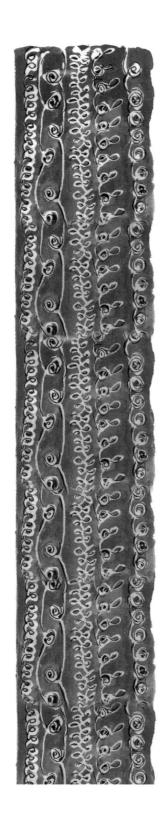

I feel fortunate to know all these villagers intimately, and I feel honoured to be welcomed as a family member and to be acquainted with such a life style. This hamlet lives in much the same way as their ancestors lived before Partition, a way of life which I first experienced during my visit in 1975.

All the houses are bhungas and are either round or rectangular, made in the traditional way with lath and plaster. There is no money for window frames and glass so the houses just have bars made by the branches passing through the aperture. I like the simplicity and practicality of this.

Nearly all of the houses are still thatched with thinning grass and tarpaulins stretched over the weak places. They have simple interiors, without any of the mud-work patterns and shisha-embedded decoration found in Dhordo.

The women still wear the long, embroidered top made up of the same patterns and stitches for which their community, Pathan, is known, the speciality being silver and gold thread-work. With the top, the women wear baggy Arabian Nights-style trousers, heavy silver anklets, silver necklaces and other traditional jewellery. Over their heads they wear much the same ordani as the Mutwa; this trails down and gives much grace to their moving bodies. It is also used to cover the face immediately, should an unknown man present himself.

The women pulled out a steel bed for me to sit on, with a quilt spread over it. It was some time before all the excitement subsided and I could start giving the work out. The women liked me to repeat the instructions so that they understood perfectly what to do. We worked hard, and I then suggested a tea break.

A young girl went away to make the tea and came back after some time with a tin container and some saucers. The chai was delicious, flavoured with cardamom. The girl laughed and said it had taken some time as she had had to milk the buffalo, as she had no ready milk. I think the tea was made completely with milk. It was poured out scalding hot into the saucers, and after two saucers' full I was renewed and given the energy and impetus to finish the distribution of the embroidery work. I have never had tea in a tea cup in this village: it is very possible they cannot afford them. It was good to see eight or so of us balancing the saucers

Previous page: a quietly smoking charcoal kiln outside the village Jurawada

on our fingers and managing to drink without spilling any chai. Slurping is quite acceptable.

Last year, the women in the village were not so interested in the embroidery work, as they were fully employed and suddenly prosperous due to the Government's scheme for buying all the charcoal which the villagers could make. The villagers were so industrious that, through last year's work alone, the women were able to afford gold earrings and nose-studs, which they were now all wearing. This year, the Government scheme has been stopped, so once again this little hamlet has not so much money coming in. But it is expected and hoped for that the Government will re-open the scheme.

The hamlet sees much hardship when the monsoon fails. In times past I have seen old and young, both women and men, from this hamlet having to work on the road scheme implemented by the Government at the time of famine. The rough hand grasping my own in the handshake is no foreigner to manual work.

After our tea, we sat around talking, and I distributed some drawing and writing books and pens and pencils to the children, and some reading glasses for the men and women that I had brought with me. All who had a need of glasses, or thought they might do, were busy trying them on. Then a gentleman who turned out to be their school teacher joined us. The village lacks a school for their children and has no means or vehicle to send them to the Government school. This year, several farmers from Bhuj have bought buffalo and cows for the villagers to raise. They are using some of

Left: silver embroidery
Right: striking man dressed in black from Zarawada village

this money for their children's education, and have hired a teacher who comes on a part-time basis from another hamlet.

The teacher wanted to try on the glasses I had brought, as he could not see. Every year I bring reading glasses with different magnifications to Dhordo, and this year I had many pairs and had brought a selection with me to the Pathan village. However, it became clear that the teacher had a serious eyesight problem, as none of my glasses gave him any more vision - he was virtually without sight. I thought this such a catastrophe for a teacher that I gave him the money to go to the optician in Bhuj.

Our tea, embroidery work and distribution of glasses and gifts being over, the women and I parted in warm friendship. Tired and dusty, Alladin and I reached Dhordo in the mid-afternoon. Sifyer's sister gave me a vessel of hot water and I poured the welcome liquid over myself. In a desert area, water takes on a different meaning, and becomes precious and much desired. After luxuriously washing my hair, myself and my clothes, I felt very clean, refreshed, and relaxed. So much so that I dozed off and was woken by a noise. I had left the door open and a nanny goat had managed to eat all my fruit. Well, I thought, her milk should be good, as she had eaten a big bunch of grapes, many guavas, a bunch of bananas and some nut crunch!

When I exclaimed over this to Sifyer, she laughed and said, "Lorna you are now experiencing rural life". I like this experiencing of rural life - I appreciate that it is all part of the tapestry of life in the village. Indeed, I savour the daily gambols of the goats and kids, upsetting the vessels round the houses as they tip-tap around on their petite, high-heeled hooves. The sound of their hooves, together with the bellowing of the buffalo, and chickens clucking and scratching, are some of the animal noises which make up the daily sounds. Along with these noises are the soft voices of the women, as they sit together and embroider while the children play. Sometimes I hear my name quietly called by a child from a roof, and I look up and wave.

Rural life means that Dhordo, situated many miles from city pollution, benefits from clean air and from nights with the air so transparent that

Opposite: typical gold border

*Above: Sonbai wearing her own handsome gold
and silver dress Pathan Community.*

97

the vault of the sky is a clear dome studded with bright stars. The full moon almost gives the clarity of daylight.

I like being woken up by a chorus of roosters announcing the dawn, together with the cadence of the voice of the Mullah, who wakes you with a cough through his microphone as he clears his throat before his call to prayers.

One day I found numerous children's shoes lying around in pairs all over the quiet compound in front of Sifyer's house, just as though the children had all jumped for joy at the same moment and flown off, leaving their shoes and flip flops as a silent reminder of themselves.

The children are happy with virtually no toys to play with. Their games are all improvised and imaginative. In the compound, the steel-framed beds are put out from the houses in the day time and set on their sides. This offers a great variety of pursuits. Children turn head-over-heels on the bed legs, one on each raised leg, and they convert washing set to dry over the bed's frame into houses and into sleeping places where children can be seen curled up. I saw Sifyer's daughter, Nafisa, tie the two ends of her scarf to a bed leg and sit in it, swinging to her heart's content.

An image of a child playing with a modest tea set would be Nafisa setting out a few small plastic cups and saucers and odd plastic tops as vessels onto a block of wood.

Infants are carried around and tended by siblings only a few years older. There is a metal, three-seated swing next to Sifyer's house, which is a great attraction for all of us. Many times I have seen children swinging it high. On more than one occasion I have seen between two and three children from eight to twelve years old with their one-year-old cousin in the middle. All swinging together on it, they go as high as possible with no-one holding on to the youngster, but the sturdy infant sits there keeping his balance. They expect the infant to be safe and he is.

It is a real lesson in how children of all ages play by themselves with virtually none of the toys we know most children to have in the West. I watched the children this evening, and every child went about skipping lightly. Skipping is a sign of real happiness and happier children would be hard to find.

"Happiness is also in your teeth," I was told many years ago in India. When I questioned this, the answer was, "Well, if you smile, you show your teeth". Children in Dhordo show their teeth all the time.

In Dhordo the custom is for nobody to be alone or to sleep alone. Sifyer's daughter sleeps with her paternal grandmother, who is a widow; and, similarly, a granddaughter of Mrs Gulbeg keeps her company. Another family share twins. Poppeli's daughter had twins; one twin chooses to live with Poppeli and the other with her daughter.

It is very apparent that there is a great deal of love given to all the children from everybody. In one day, each child will have spent time with at least eight children to whom it is related and will have been in at least six homes of its own family. I cannot think of more balanced and loving peo-

ple. Each infant will experience at least six mothers in one day, and at least six women and children, if not more, will have spent time holding, feeding and playing with the child. What you never hear are cross, chiding or scolding voices, and the children never seem to misbehave.

The daily round for the village women and girls comprises the preparing and making of food, organising water for household needs, washing clothes, tending the animals, if the household has any, and embroidering.

The woman will also pay attention to her religion, and when the mosque gives out the call to prayers, she will halt her work, take out her prayer mat and, facing Mecca, say her prayers. If the ladies are busy with small children then it is a cursory halt. But religion is a very present part of each day's rhythm and order. The day is interwoven with the five daily calls to prayer. Women practise their religion in their homes, while it is only the men who attend the mosque - which they do every evening.

The main task of the morning is drawing the household water. Miaw Hussein, the headman, has had Government water piped to the houses. The Government rations the water supply to a delivery time of a quarter of an hour. The water comes on at seven o'clock and is left on to fill bucket after bucket, which is emptied into large, plastic water butts set around the compound. After this routine, morning chai is made, household chores accomplished, and then clothes washed. Washing may not be done every day but is carried out frequently through the week. Girls and women go to the well to draw water and do the washing early in the morning.

The well water is pulled up in two yellow plastic containers which have a rope attached and which are lowered, filled, hauled up, and poured into the water pots. The girls and women come from every direction and go away in chattering twos and threes, balancing the vessels without seeming effort.

I love going to the well and watching the girls coming to and fro - a daily vision of delight. They come with two pots on their head and often with a third pot under their arm. The sun glints on the bright steel of the pots; and the girls with their bright flowing clothes and the trailing ordanies are a beautiful sight.

I found this a very attractive subject not only to observe but to draw, and would often be found there. The women drew water and I drew them! It is a difficult subject as the person is in continual movement, so you have to work fast and accurately in order to catch the essence of the movement and colour.

I would quietly leave the house, taking a plastic chair with me and my small back-pack of art materials, and set up, only up to be discovered and have chai brought to me. It was always in a blue enamel cup with a steel saucer ever the top to stop flies and dust. If the buffalo were lingering in front of me, one of the children gathered around me would shoo them away with a thorny branch torn from the acacia tree behind me.

A typical scene in the morning when women came to the well to wash cloths

I also made many drawings of the women washing clothes. I consider the time spent here a great pleasure.

I had forgotten that there was a Harijan enclave at Dhordo, until one day a brilliantly bedecked, gorgeous bevy of them came to the well. They were all wearing their traditional attire, which is in striking contrast to the Mutwa, the two communities' outfits being markedly different.

They were in full, brightly embroidered, long tops, the embroidery inset with large shisha mirrors flashing like signals of Morse code. Under the tops were worn full skirts with shiny, stiff, brocade borders, which made the skirts stick out. The same stiff brocade hid their faces from view, as it was used to edge their head-covering. This bulky piece of fabric was held in place in a great bunch under their arms. These women were quite happy for me to photograph them, unlike the Mutwa, who do not allow photography.

When I came in 1975, every day in the morning after the chores, and again in the afternoon after dinner, you would see all the women and girls from eight years upwards sitting and embroidering. The young girls would be learning from their mothers, and all would be working hard. The afternoons were very social, with the women sitting in great clusters and breaking the hours with the passing round of the chai kettle. Most women in those days embroidered for up to eight hours.

Now, the children go to school and many women do not embroider, or if they do it is often commercial work. The social side of the learned oral teaching of the craft and tradition of Mutwa embroidery has been broken down, and now only one or two women will be seen sitting together for short periods sewing.

After seeing the Harijans, I discovered on my evening walk the Harijan enclave - and in fact remembered it from 1975. The composition of the community was the same, with the houses set in a rectangle around an open centre, but now the houses are more numerous, former gaps being filled with new bhungas. In 1975 the Harijan women were employed by the Mutwa for domestic work (which is still the case) and to build their houses (using traditional mud work).

Wherever I was working in the village someone would appear with my tea in this blue cup with the small saucer covering it to keep out dust and flies.

At that time, too, the men made very good chappels, or sandals. I saw no evidence this time of this traditional leather work for which the Harijan is known. But I did see some fine, robust embroidery. The neat enclave is a little way out from the village and next to the camel corps.

I made an enjoyable visit to them, and continued to visit the camel corps policemen. I like visiting the camel men and sometimes go to draw the camels and have tea. One man I drew this evening was Hari, a big, burly man whose home in Haryana is some 1,200 kilometres away. He always refers to my drawing and paintings as "smart art"! He has a rough, quite ugly face with a great smile and a large, bushy moustache with an elaborate curl at the ends, such a one as all Rajasthani men used to wear until quite recently, when they suddenly went out of fashion.

The camel corps policemen are permanently billeted in Dhordo. The village is right beside the Rann, which forms the border between India and Pakistan. As there is no alert between Pakistan and India at this time in 2009, it must be a lonely and boring posting for just three men. The border is patrolled in two frontier positions: one on the edge of the salt Rann and the other fifteen miles into the Rann. I understand Hari's duty is to patrol midway between these two frontiers at one a.m. each night.

A distinctive badge of a racing camel on the uniform informs you that these men are serving in the camel corps.

I was proudly shown a camel which smokes cigarettes - questionable fun but fascinating! I sketched the camels and, on my walk back, passed the road sign to the village, which always brings a smile to my face: "Left Hand Cruve". This sign is one of several on the road from Birendira, obviously written by the same person who got the u and the r the wrong way round.

I see rural life in Dhordo as a tapestry, which with its customs, people, and many traditions making the threads of the tapestry, has achieved something ever-changing, rich and vibrant.

Wrestlers at Gradara

Chapter 6

Wrestling

I became aware of village sports playing a significant role in the life of the villagers when I was shown videos from the kinsmen of Dhordo, who since Partition now live in Sindh. These videos portrayed wrestling and horse races. I realised I had seen horses being raced and bred many times over the years I had visited Dhordo. The horses are a special breed called Mewar and have the distinction of twisting and swivelling their ears when listening so that the tips touch. The horse is ridden with the reins held tight, so that its head is held up at full gallop.

Village sports are a welcome diversion in the year's calendar, and in Banni several programmes are played each year. The itinerary usually includes horse and camel racing and a livestock show, besides wrestling matches.

Having heard of my interest, Mr Jethi, the curator of Ana Mahal, found a wrestling venue for me taking place at Gradasia on the 14th September. I made a special journey to be there and stayed in Mandvi, as the venue was not many kilometres distant. It was arranged that Alladin would travel down from Dhordo and collect Pramood Jethi. Pramood Jethi and Alladin arrived about mid-day and we found our host, who was known to Alladin. He was the organiser of the occasion, which was to celebrate and honour the holy Muslim pir who was buried there. Our host had arranged a fair and the wrestling contest. We parked the cars and walked through the fair, which had very good attendance. There were many stalls selling sweets and namkin, balloons, toys and other attractions.

First, we were shown into a tent, where I mistakenly presumed the wrestling would take place, as it had a ring around which we all stood. In the ring were a donkey and a man who called out to the audience that the donkey would go and stand next to the foreigners. The donkey stood right in front of me. Then it was told to look for the lady in an orange sari; it quietly walked round to where she stood. The next command was for it to stand by the lady with the very bright lipstick. Many absurdities were called for and each time the donkey did as was asked of it. This provided a very light-hearted exhibition. None of us could fathom out how the donkey did it, or what or when a signal was given.

The fair comprised several different types of merry-go-rounds and numerous stalls with sweets and restaurant set-ups, with vendors of sugar cane juice, snacks of every description, chai wallahs and fresh juice stalls...There were sellers of pipes, huge bunches of bright balloons, and je-jaws of every description.

The fair took place on a hill, so we walked through the fair to the top, and were seated by our host under the banyan tree next to the shrine of the Muslim holy man, in whose memory the festival was given. As we sat, we counted many more Hindus than Muslims bringing gifts to honour the pir. Hindus are greater in number here and in these country areas both Muslim holy men and Hindu gods are revered by both religious communities. The shrine was honoured, as Hindu shrines or deities are, with gifts of coconut and sweets (or prasad). Steel tumblers of coconut milk were poured out for us prepared from some of the coconut offerings.

WRESTLING

After lunch at the local restaurant, we drove by a circular route to the top of the fair, where we found a tight-rope act in full swing. It was a family of entertainers: one beat the drum while another rang a steel tali, making a stirring noise, and a third told us what was going to happen. A delicate young girl of no more than eight years was the star, her slight body in her short, frilled dress tense as she walked with bare feet from one support to the other, balancing with her pole. Then she was set one task after another. The first was to walk with a pot on her head, the next to rock the rope from side to side in the middle when walking barefoot and afterwards with her shoes on and then to walk with a steel plate under one foot - jumping it along while she stood in it. Lastly, she walked on the rope while turning a steel wheel with her feet. When she had accomplished her last feat she turned a somersault onto the ground and skipped about collecting her coins, once more a child of eight.

After watching these feats, we walked to the venue for the wrestling, where our host again very kindly got us chairs under the shade of a tree. In front of us was a ring chalked out, with people carefully picking the small stones out from the sandy earth, so that the wrestlers would have a soft landing. A set of musicians opposite us started to drum and chant while everyone found a place. We were outside the top of the hill fort with the ring in front, facing the fort wall.

Gradually all the ring around us was filled with a thick throng of people at least ten deep, all sitting. Opposite were two high fort walls on two levels, one in front of the other. First the lower wall filled with a line of people sitting with their legs dangling over the high wall and then the even higher wall filled with a human fringe. In this precarious position, and in response to the proceedings below, the fringed wall with its human cargo would dangerously move and sway. To our left, the ground rose up and was filled with people. At the top was a lorry and this too was filled with people standing in the truck and sitting on the top of the cab. Every part of the compound was filled with spectators: even the trees behind us had been invaded by small boys, such was the interest in the sport.

A master of ceremonies executed some warrior cut-and-thrust movements with his sword to the beating of the drums, while policemen with lathis (or long sticks) took up threatening positions - so the crowd knew not to get out of order. Gradually, one became aware of young men around the ring straightening their trousers and vests.

Then one wrestler stood in the centre, holding a long scarf patterned in the colours of madder and indigo, in what appeared to me to be an Ajrakh print. A white-clad official took this scarf from the contestant, twisting it and then winding it tight twice round the wrestler's waist. To allow this, the contestant had to lift his vest up to his armpits. The twisted band was tightened fully, then knotted, and the knot placed to the back.

The opponent was similarly dealt with. Then, with vests uplifted, the combatants inspected each other, circled each other and gracefully moved their opponent's waistband knot to where they wanted it. This grace and movement gradually developed into a full grip on each other until they were fully engaged. Each tried to get his leg under the other's so that he could lift him off his feet by raising him by his waistband.

Combatants had different ploys for winning. There were two burly young men who gripped each other like blacksmiths at a mediaeval fair. When one finally threw the other to the ground, he dropped his full weight on him to hold him down, so making sure of success.

The tension in the crowd is heightened by the drumming of the musicians, who bring the tussle to a height of excitement. Then, when you least expect it, one man will throw the other onto his back, and it is all over.

The wrestlers all wear very loose pants, the fullness gathered together with a cord passing through the waistband. The loose folds are then pulled up through and over the waistband, which is below the twisted scarf. This is done to free the knees so greater movement is gained for the wrestler.

I drew the combatants in their graceful circling and gentle initial embrace - drawings which reminded me of the figures which you find on Greek vases. The movements of the wrestlers' bodies and the folds of their garments perfectly replicate these early Greek images. Alexander of Macedonia passed through this land, and it could be that he introduced the game from Greece. To dispel the fatigues of constant battle, Alexander put on many games for the men, and wrestling was one of them. The martial art of wrestling is referred to in the Iliad in the Trojan wars, which took place in the 13th and 12th centuries BC.

Interestingly, I have found the following report of a wrestling match given by our friend Marianne Postans, who wrote this account of a wrestling match to which she was invited by his Highness the Rao of Cutch in 1834.

'In the hall of audience in the Aina Mahal his Highness - "Will't please you to go see the wrestlers", is, in other words, the Rao's general invitation to his guests; and he at once leads them to a carpeted and draperied balcony, looking over the courts of the palace, which are

I worked at great speed to catch
the movement of the wrestlers.
All the drawings were done on the spot.

111   WRESTLING

WRESTLING

Sizing each other up!

crowded by anxious spectators. Behind his Highness's chair stand slaves, gracefully waving punkas of ostrich and peacock feathers round his superbly ornamented turban; and below him are ranged the wrestlers, fine Rajpoots, in the prime of life, displaying a symmetry of form and a development of muscular power, not unworthy the gymnasium theatres of ancient Greece. If we accept one long waving lock of hair, their heads were closely shaven, and their only covering a pair of crimson silk drawers, descending about half way down to the knee, and bound tightly round the loins with a many-coloured scarf.

After a succession of salaams to the Rao, two of the wrestlers step forward, and the exhibition commences, by each violently slapping the inside of his arms and thighs, in succession, with the open palm of the opposite hand; until at an understood signal, then men seize each other by the waist, place their foreheads together, and struggling, toss, and twist each other about, until one falls, then the victor, cheered by the spectators. gracefully lifts a handful of dust to his forehead, and salaaming to the Rao, backs to his place, while another pair step forward to repeat the same ceremony.'

- and she goes on to make the comment that yet,

'meagre as it was, the display seemed eminently attractive to the crowd around us, who rent the air with shouts of applause, and evinced the most barbarous, and unfeigned delight during the combats.'

Mrs Postans not only gives us a rich glimpse of the royal court in the 1830s but also shows the game played in the same manner as I have witnessed here at Gradasia some one hundred and seventy years later. She, too, was reminded of the Grecian games, but above all she recounts the same hearty enjoyment of the game by the spectators!

Looking back at India's history of the game, we have a description in the Mahabharata of an encounter between the accomplished wrestlers Bhima and Jarasabdha. So, was the game here already in India or did it come from Greece?

On another close subject, it has been suggested that the sari evolved after Alexander the Great came to India. There is an undeniable similarity between the folded ancient Grecian clothes and the folded Indian clothes; neither culture employs tailoring.

We might never know the answer to these questions, but we do know that wrestling is a celebrated, age-old sport and that the grace of present-day combatants is as much a delight for us to watch now as it has been over the centuries. This was one of my best days in India - watching India enjoying itself.

Waiting his turn.

Beautifully caparisoned horse.

Chapter 7

Mekan Dada

Knowing of my interest in wrestling, Alladin told me of one of Kutch's most important saints, Mekan Dada. A fair dedicated to his memory is held annually at the place of his shrine. Alladin said that I could attend his shrine and see not only more wrestling but horse and camel racing as well.

The shrine of this Hindu saint is near the village of Dhrang, just below Banni in a large, airy valley. It is one of Kutch's most important sacred shrines and is a place of great pilgrimage, revered by both Hindu and Muslim. Such is the volume of pilgrims, that there is a hostel (or daramsala) for people to stay in. The festival held each year is a three-day event and commences on the eve of the full moon in February, which is also the eve of Shivrati (the Great Night of Shiva).

The temple which holds Mekan Dada's shrine has been recently rebuilt and now presents a brightly painted series of temple spires and domed buildings. The innermost shrine holds a large mound of ashes from a perpetual fire which has burnt in Mekan Dada's memory since his departure from life. People often take a pinch of the ashes, as they are believed to benefit the recipient.

Mekan Dada was born in 1666 and lived until 1729. This was a time of strong religious fervour, and Mekan Dada developed, during a time of secluded meditation in Dhrang, a yogic meditation practice to develop powerful spiritual energy. He is ever since revered as a saint due both to his holiness and his good works.

Dhrang is adjacent to the Salt Rann of Kutch. Over this salt-marsh waste many people journeyed from Kutch to Sindh and from Sindh to Kutch. Families and kin lived on either side of the Rann, and trade and commerce flowed both ways. The width of the Rann varies from one part to another. It is a salt marsh, with the residue of salt lying heavier and forming a white field in some areas, while in others it creates islands of salt marsh. Though two hundred years ago before the earthquake of 1819, when the Arabian sea began to cover the Rann the salt would not have been as heavy and create such a continuous field of white as it does today. The marsh is treacherous to cross and was in the time of Mekan Dada largely an unmapped area. Even now, without the aid of compass and map, it presents the same dangers. Having travelled in the Rann for only a kilometre or two, one encounters a featureless expanse, with interspersed fields of white. Under the tropical sun it becomes a great hazard for the unprepared traveller.

In the past, many people lost their way and suffered hardship as they ran out of food and, more importantly, water. Mekan Dada had an ass and a dog. On the back of the ass he carried panniers of water and food, and he trained the dog to sniff and track down the lost travellers. The dog became so accomplished that finally he would seek and find his targets without the aid or direction of Mekan Dada. This Indian story obviously matches its Swiss counterpart of St Bernard.

Mekan Dada endeavoured through a life of yogic practice to attain the highest level of concentrated meditation. His quest was for complete control over bodily functions and the distractions of consciousness. This yogic state is known as Samadhi. Gurus teach that Samadhi is the only reality. All else is ever-changing and will not bring everlasting peace and happiness.

Mekan Dada made a conscious choice to achieve Samadhi. Following this practice, a pit would be dug at the time of approaching death, the dying person would be placed upright in it, sometimes with a terracotta water pot placed over the head, and then the body would be covered up. He would then roll his tongue, as a dog will do, to the back of his mouth, thereby closing it. The spirit was then believed to depart through the top of the head.

Mekan Dada would have been in deep meditation at the time of his interment and been practising what is described as "leaving the body." Yogis are said to attain the final liberation after leaving their bodies at the time of death. It is believed that at this time "the soul knows a complete and unbroken union with the divine, and, being free from the limitations of the body, merges effortlessly into the transcendent self". This is Great Samadhi, which is the term used for this final absorption into the Self at the time of death.

After Mekan Dada became a Great Samadhi, his mother followed the same practice at another place, and his brother, who had converted to the Muslim belief, also departed in this manner near to Mekan Dada at Dhrang. Both brothers' shrines are in Dhrang, as well as the shrines of many people who over a period of time followed this practice and committed Samadhi at Dhrang. You see their commemorative stones in great numbers round the temples.

These shrines still hold great power for people and draw to themselves both Hindu and Muslim from all over the area, as both religions hold them dear. At Gadhasia, where I saw the marvellous wrestling, the holy man was a Muslim, while here in Dhrang Maken Dada is a Hindu holy man. The same reverence is given to both Muslim and Hindu faiths. It must be remembered that, under the Moguls, who brought the Islamic faith to India, and up until Partition, Indian society

Previous page: a caparisoned Mewar horse.

Right: handsome Banni herdsmen with his red beard. Both men and women often use henna on grey hair. It is a belief among them that the henna keeps the head cool and is good for health.

116

was made up of Muslim and Hindu living with mutual respect for each other in a close–knit, intertwined society.

The first two days of the festival to mark Mekan Dada's life and death are dedicated to temple rituals and celebrations, and the third day is a sports day. The spiritual nature of the festival draws great numbers of people. Many participants turn the journey into a pilgrimage by walking for days to attend the celebrations: such is the fervent belief in the Saint's powers. The sports day draws still further spectators and in addition the participants for the various sporting contests.

On this occasion, we were to see the three most important sports: wrestling, camel-racing and the special horse races so close to the villagers' hearts.

Alladin had driven from Dhordo village and collected me from Bhuj before going on to Dhrang. We arrived to find the wrestling in full swing. Dhrang is set in a flat, sandy area surrounded on two sides by a sweep of low hills and skirted with a fringe of green trees. A very pleasant aspect.

When I had seen wrestling before in Gadhasia, we had been seated by the wall of the town's fort, which offered good views but at high risk of danger to the people sitting on it. This time at Drang, the area being flat, the wrestling was ringed by lorries, which offered grandstand views. The lorries provided three different viewing heights: the bonnet, the top of the cabin and the lorry itself. People sat or stood on all levels. The dense ring of different-sized lorries

Locally made windmills

was fronted by most of the spectators, who stood at least six-deep, while those in front of them sat down to watch. The bobbing, black heads from the serried ranks of spectators on the packed lorries, and the loud bursts of exultant cries as a wrestler brought his opponent down, held all the same excitement as at Gadhasia. Again, the same grace and beauty of the youthful wrestlers was displayed - each skirting and finally embracing the other for the grim clasp, heave, and destined fall of the opponent. The subsequent gasp, and then the cheering and roar of the crowd for the winner, expressed the magic of this martial art for all of us.

After the wrestling, there was a lull in the proceedings, as it was lunch-time and the racing was not due to start till three o'clock. Before these events, Alladin and I took a walk around the fair. We were attracted by a crowd and walked over to see a prancing horse which performed various tricks in a ring, to the amusement of the jostling onlookers. It was a pearly white horse with a red harness, he looked very fine. He danced round with tight, neat steps and then, to the thrill of all, he stood on his hind legs and presented a heroic aspect. As the horse pranced about, the crowd surged suddenly to get away from his moving, prancing body. This caused the mass of people to move as one in a ripple of movement, the potential danger causing great excitement.

I liked this fair better than the more organised big fair of Gadhasia. This was a very simple, lo-cal event with no great pretensions. There were just two inflated castles with figures on the top offering slides for the children, a simple merry-go-round for small children and a swing, shaped like a boat, which held about nine children at a time. There were no big roundabouts, dippers or other mechanical thrills.

We came across a traditional toy made for little children. It consists of a metal rod some two feet long, one end bent in a loop for a handle and the other end having a short axle with two wheels attached. This is a toy I have known since I first came to India and have seen many children over the years running about with, making the wheels turn fast as they propel it around. It is reminiscent of Victorian times, when simple toys such as a whip and top and running with a wheel and a stick to make it go were sufficient for a child's happiness. So, for fifteen rupees I bought one for Alladin's small daughter. I saw many people clutching up to twelve of these toys: obviously they are as popular as ever.

Two brilliant orange umbrellas, embroidered all over with gold and glittering in the sunlight, announced a long stall of animal equipment. Alladin told me that the traders came from Rajasthan (which accounts for the gaudy umbrellas). These were set high, one at each end of the stall; it was doing brisk business, and was obviously the reason the traders had come so far. As those attending the function were local men who for the most part earned their living from horse, goat, buffalo, cow, sheep and camel, the traders had a captive market.

Saddles were piled on the floor, while next to them were stacked four-pointed decorated covers to go under the saddle, making a fine display on a horse. They were worked with embroidery and felt-work or patches of coloured leather-work. Above were racks of halters and

MEKAN DADA

An Ahir girl pays
close attention to the
syrup being poured
over her crushed ice
locally called Gola

horse reins, and so forth. Next came cascades of beaded necklaces for the horse and then there were more beaded necklaces for bullocks, cows, buffalo and goat. When I first was here, the beads for the buffalo and cow were in big globs of coloured glass, spun in a crude but beautiful fashion in mostly blue and green, and were strung on knotted home-made coloured string. Now, there are plastic beads threaded onto bright nylon. But Indians are a decorative people and they will decorate anything and turn it into a sparkling colourful item.

It was good to witness a country man in white turban and lungi with large gold earrings buying many pieces, counting and choosing the different-coloured, beaded necklaces. He was working out if he had a necklace for each animal and he then went on to choose a bell for each necklace. He was carefully choosing different sized bells, as he would then not only know where each animal was, but by its different sound know which animal it was. We were attracted by the throng and by the vibrant voices of hucksters selling items from the backs of lorries and small vehicles. Just like the barrow boys of Petticoat Lane and the East-End of London, they were auctioning off cheap wares such as clocks and glittering glass dishes and vases.

We moved on to see peanuts being roasted over a fire. The peanuts were put in a wide oval dish like a big wok, mixed with sand, which raised the temperature, and were turned over with a disc of metal. Within the rim was a mesh, like a big tea strainer. When the nuts were sufficiently roasted, the trader sieved out the sand, with many high tossings onto newspaper, and made cones for the nuts. They tasted very good: crunchy, and hot and holding no gritty residues.

Next we came to a tasty dish which I had not eaten for a long time, namely corn crisps and gram nuts tossed in a newspaper cone with chopped onion and a good squeeze of lemon over them.

Three Mewar horses at the races note their swivel ears

Sharp and crisp at the same time.

Several stalls were selling green grapes, the fruit packed so solidly it made a wall of green, which only on closer inspection could be recognized as grapes.

Fruit-salad sellers announced themselves by the pile of ankle-deep thick peelings surrounding their stalls. The passing buffalo and goat would have a feast the next day eating the pickings. The stallholders were mostly selling red watermelons and pineapples cut into thin slices, sprinkled over with a chai Masala and served in small dishes, to be eaten by hand.

Sugarcane was stacked like graceful palm fronds and was guarded by a robust lady wielding a big axe. On demand by the buyer she cut the cane into bundles some eighteen inches long. Women were her main customers and were to be seen leaving with big bundles of cane. Nearby was another stall selling cane; here, the vendor was peeling the cane and then chopping it into small lengths for immediate consumption. This is a very popular snack, and people were to be seen everywhere chewing the cane, sucking out the sugar and spitting out the residue.

We sat down for a very good chai, and Alladin told me we were mostly seeing Ahir women. This area is below Banni and, while the menfolk were from all over the region, including several from Dhordo village, the women were mostly from the surrounding Dhrang area. This area is predominantly settled by Hindu and abounds in the community of Ahir, and it is commonly known as an Ahir festival. The women in Banni will not go to such fairs, being in a self-imposed purdah. They will say to me, "Lorna, it is our custom", and they seem perfectly happy in this.

Ahir

I was truly amazed and saddened by my re-introduction to the Ahir community. Now I did not recognise them by their dress. I knew the Ahir well from my first visit in 1975 and from subsequent visits, when all the women wore their embroidered traditional dress, of which I have many fine examples in my collection. Ahir traditionally wore a choli top, which is gathered under the bust, and often with a long narrow pocket for keeping rupees in. This top is heavily embroidered in chain-stitch and has large shisha mirrors stitched into it. Roundels of embroidery inset with sparkling large shisha mirrors circle each breast, giving an armoured, while attractive and womanly, appearance. Ahir favour yellow and white embroidery, mostly in chain-stitch onto a green background. The choli is a backless top with a string tied across the middle of the bare back to secure it. Worn with this is a large gathered dark skirt, and round the bottom is a thick band of embroidery, embroidered in the same matching colours and motifs as the top. To cover the head and bare back, a long, dark ordani is worn. This was made from hand-woven wool (Indian sheep have a short staple which is wiry to the touch). It was tie-dyed with a dark orange or red onto a dark brown or black ground, and was often embroidered along the ends, again in the same colours with the large shisha-work.

*Ahir woman and child, note her communities
earrings and her big bangle, in 1975 it was
made from ivory, now it had been replaced with
plastic and is rouged at the time of marriage.*

A joyeous lady with her
daughter at the fair

On this occasion I struggled to identify these Ahir women. I perceived they were wearing the same shaped garments, but without the embroidery. They had the long dark skirt, sans embroidery, and the tops were fashioned in mostly the same design, but now made up from diverse fabrics. These were often sequinned or made up from pre-embroidered, glittering lengths of fabric in all sorts of colours and designs. Here and there were tops without decoration but in the original green colour. On their heads, the women were now wearing ordanis made from printed cotton in tie-dye patterns.

I think it is some ten years since the time of my last visit to the Ahir community, when the women were mostly wearing their traditional dress. I can foresee that in a few years the dress will have utterly vanished, so fast is the abandonment of their community identity. Even the shadow of identity which I now see will be gone.

The older men whom I now saw at the fair were for the most part still wearing more traditional clothes: the white lungi and the long top with a large white turban, and often to be seen was the Ajrakh scarf, now worn as a scarf or wound into a turban rather than a lungi.

To return to my day at the sports: after my chai, I went back to the car to eat lunch, while Alladin went off to meet his friends and have some Indian fare. He parted from me with the words which are a joke among the locals: "Oh, you look solemn and without a smile - you must have been to a fair!" As I ate my lunch, I watched the bright women and children pile into rickshaws and small lorries, clutching their bundles of sugar cane and other small purchases. The afternoon affair of sport is a man's province. As far as I could see, I and two other women were the only females present.

Over the next hour, I watched a cavalcade of motorbikes, each bike mounted with two to three passengers, weaving their way through the sand-dunes in front of me and disappearing into the landscape. These motorbikes were interspersed with lorries laden with men, rocking to and fro as the vehicles swung from side to side over the uneven terrain, and with cars of all descriptions and sizes. And lastly foot passengers, heads swathed in scarves against the dust kicked up by the vehicles, all making their way in the same direction.

Alladin came back, chewing on a piece of sugar cane. Our car then joined the rocking procession of vehicles travelling to the venue for the races. We entered onto a dried, cracked river bed, which was where the races were to be held. Flat and wide, it offered the ideal race track. It went on for as far as the eye could see in both directions, and, even though I had seen many vehicles make their way there, I found the volume of people totally unexpected. This was a densely packed audience of many thousands of men and boys lining both sides of the river bed. It was a convivial time: friends were meeting each other with much back-slapping and hearty welcomes.

A number of the older men wore beards of biblical proportions, some of which were hennaed bright red. Around men's heads were wound not only white turbans and Ajrakh turbans but also floral-printed scarves and checked cloths, and here and there the crocheted cap of the Muslim man favoured more by city dwellers. The youths all wore Western dress. They have long since abandoned traditional wear.

We found Abdul Karim, who suggested the place from which we should watch the games. We were also met by Turki, a great friend of the deceased Shri Gulbeg. We parked next to him, and Alladin and I shared some delicious slices of papaya, which dripped from our fingers.

Turki has his name from his forefathers, who came to Kutch from Turkey and settled here some four hundred years back. The solidarity of the community is so strong that Turki and his family are still in touch with their Turkish kinsmen four hundred years later, and trade currently goes on between them to the satisfaction of both communities. This community in Kutch live in one village and marry only within their community, which means they are very limited in their marriage opportunities. I suspect that, as India is changing in so many ways, this restriction will become relaxed and the members of the community will spread and marry Muslims outside their community. This has happened in the case of the headman of Birendira village, where his community was so reduced that there was no-one of marriageable age. He therefore broke with tradition and married within the village a woman from another Muslim community.

The day was wonderfully sunny but not too hot, with a fresh breeze, making it a lovely spot to watch the races from. Although we were just half a kilometre from the fair, the landscape was very different: we were in a dry river bed with the yellow sand stretching to the horizon on both sides. Facing us were the green acacia trees fringing the edge of the course, and behind them the undulating blue hills. A sparkling day full of humour and conviviality.

I gave my phone camera to Alladin and appointed him cameraman. We saw some of the horses amongst the crowd being saddled and prepared with fine equipage, and horsemen getting their steeds ready for the off by racing them briefly here and there. The horses were well got up: some had their manes embellished and tasselled with decorated harnesses and embroidered covers.

The horses are small in stature and the strain is originally Arab. The breed is called Mewar and is very highly prized. It is a costly enterprise not only to buy a horse but to then maintain it, so it is only the wealthier village man who can afford one. The Mewar horse is bred in many colours and here I saw a piebald of pure white and black, very strikingly marked. Another was of a very pale, soft honey colour with a darker hue on the ears, which added a delicate attractiveness to it. There

Mewar horses racing at
Mekan Dada.

was also a black horse which had blue in the black, and then there was wonderful horse with a glossy coat the colour of dark, rich chocolate.

We were alerted to the first race, which was the camel race, by tiny specks in the distance. For the camels it is a long race, started some five miles back in the riverbed. Some riders had dropped out when they saw the three leaders so far ahead. The first camel raced by with great, loping strides. I was surprised to see that the camel rider sitting so far back appeared to be riding without a saddle. He had very long reins and, as he had no stirrups to steady him, it must have made controlling the camel difficult. The camel is an exceptional creature with its unique running style. It was not quite Lawrence of Arabia but it was very good fun, and the second and third contestants came hard on the first contestant's heels. We all roared our enthusiasm and happiness for the riders.

Then followed an interval where we were moved aside once or twice by a patrolling police car which veered down our side, sweeping the spectators back and making the track bigger again for the forthcoming horse races.

Once more, this started out with specks in the distance, that seemed to appear out of the ether as thundering horses which raced by so fast it was hard to take it all in. It was a vision of beautiful, fine horses reined in so that they were stepping quickly and delicately but not at a gallop. Against the ochre-dust river bed, the colourful riders on their jewel-bright horses with their reins and rich caparisoned covers stood out magnificently.

We cheered at the spectacle, and the judges' vehicle rushed past in tandem with the first rider. The judges have to be very alert because if the rider does not ride his steed in the correct fashion he is disqualified. At the same time they must observe the second and third riders also; so if one is disqualified then the second must also have been seen to be ridden properly.

There were about five races in all, some with the horses being ridden at full gallop. Then came the grand finale for the biggest prize. Here, the first rider of this most important race was so happy to be the winner and was so well ahead of the second contender that, on the final approach, he suddenly flung his arms wide, stretching his body and arching his

*Good example of traditional
Ahir top circa 1975*

MEKAN DADA

back into a bow in ecstatic and exuberant triumph. We cheered him high, so great was our happiness for him.

We were a joyous crowd slowly saying our farewells. While I was saying good-bye to Turki and his menfolk, an invitation was extended to me to attend a wedding in his village in a few days' time. We got into our various vehicles and made our way back through the dunes, with sand and dust settling everywhere. Somehow we did not mind this final dusting, as if it was a benevolent god giving us absolution, perhaps a blessing cast down on us by Mekan Dada himself.

When we got back to the fairground, Alladin suddenly halted the car and sprang out. In a couple of minutes he was back, but quite changed in appearance. He had bought himself a leather hat, an Indian look-alike to the famous Australian koubra. My friend and guide was suddenly transformed into an Indian Australian. He said he had had his eye on the hat, and had suddenly made his mind up. I hope his daughter liked her father's new appearance and also enjoyed the metal-wheeled toy. Many people left Dhrang fair in a happy mood that evening, including myself.

Postcript: two years later in February 2012 I visited the fair of Mekan Dada again. I chose to go on the first day, when I observed the Ahir in their masses and noted the following amendments to their costume.

I was informed that on the first day of the fair the Ahir men dance and also, but separately,

Ahir woman showing her bare back. This traditionally cut blouse is the same as in 1975 but has less embroidery. She is wearing the huge bracelet now made from plastic.

so do the women. Indeed it was so, it presented a very different experience and a very different atmosphere from my previous visit: it is truly a ladies' day. Ahir women and children of all ages were here in vast numbers and were almost the only community to be seen. On the sports days, you see several communities represented as the events draw a different selection of spectators.

Women of all ages were standing in a big ring at least three deep, with more women and their children sitting in front to watch the men dance. Although the women were not in the complete attire of years before, it was clear that they were wearing what has now evolved into the present-day traditional Ahir costume. The women all wore a choli top, and again it was worn with the long skirt mainly in black, with a long ordani head-covering, but this varied in colour and design from the strict black of former years. Many of the women's choli tops were worked with traditional embroidery on the bottom edge and sides, but now leaving the breast plain. Moreover, the women still adhered to the backless top fastened by two strings tied in a bow, and they were proudly wearing the single huge bracelet, now in plastic as against the former ivory. Some women even had the correct three earrings of former years, these being a long silver length with a cube at the end.

They presented a very fine and arresting body of men and women. It seems the women like to come to these two fair days much more than to the sports events. They enjoy watching the dancing, listening to the music with the deafening but hypnotic beat of the drums, visiting the temple, paying their respects to the memory of Mekan Dada, and wandering round the fair having snacks and making small purchases.

Two years ago I had observed with dismay the decline in the wearing of the traditional apparel and had predicted its rapid disappearance. However, I now saw that the women are still proudly wearing a semblance of Ahir costume. This is their tradition today, and it is flourishing.

Chapter 8

Tea with His Highness

As the village of Dhordo was within the Kingdom of the former state of Kutch, it raised questions which I wished to discuss with His Highness, Maharao Shi Pragmuji. In 1975, one of my letters of introduction had introduced me to the present Maharajah's father, and since that time I have on occasion met his present Highness, sometimes together with my son. Now, in January 2010, I found I still had His Highness Maharao Shi Pragmuji's telephone number, and on ringing Ranjit Palace was invited to come for tea.

On getting down from the rickshaw I walked through the formal gardens which surround the red sandstone Edwardian palace, which is His Highness's residence in Bhuj. The tracery of birds' feet could be clearly seen in the long, finely-swept earth paths which led me to the palace steps. Here I was met by a waiting, very deferential, elderly servant. I was conducted to a formal sitting room, where the sparse natural light, even when combined with the dim electric lighting, kept the room in a twilight condition. After the fierce clarity of the four-in-the-afternoon Indian sun, I could barely see anything.

By the time His Highness entered, my eyes had had time to adjust and I found myself sitting in a carefully kept sitting room which has stayed crystallised from the days of Partition and the British Raj. I have experienced similar rooms in many stately Indian palaces, all of which were built at the turn of the nineteenth century.

I love the quiet of rooms such as the one I was ushered into; they seem to have a stillness and timeless quality. I can easily imagine the Maharajah for whom the palace was originally built gliding into the room in silk-slippered shoes. He would have been a magnificent sight in his opulent finery, with full-skirted, embroidered robes, a jewelled dagger at his side, and strings of pearls round his neck, and more pearls and jewels decorating his full silk turban. Maharajahs loved jewels and were particularly fond of pearls. His Highness and his equally richly dressed family might well have been entertaining members of the Residence, who would have been in their Edwardian clothes and would have looked appropriate against the English architecture

and furniture designed for English people at this period. The opposite elements of the two cultures would be having a meeting point in this and similar rooms throughout the Raj.

While the Raj influenced and changed the buildings of India's royal families, the incumbents were still clad in their traditional clothes, but sitting on chairs, having abandoned their floor-seated culture. It was as though the jewel, being the rajah, had been set in the wrong design, as they seem to be at variance and in great and interesting contrast with their new surroundings.

On the furniture and walls there are often displayed handsome black and white photographs of previous maharajahs, and sometimes also of British sovereigns. These give another rich glimpse into the life lived then. Fine oil portrait paintings of earlier rajahs and their consorts, as well as others depicting common topics such as hunting and wildlife, have been collected and displayed. Carpets with large floral designs fill most of the floor space and make the rooms very quiet, muting voices and sounds to a quiet cadence.

The rooms invariably have high ceilings, which gives coolness. The tall doors have glass in the upper portion, which is often etched with the royal monogram, and lets what little natural light there is into the room. This room was no exception in all its accoutrements. I always enjoy the peacefulness and civility that these rooms present. The gravity of the rooms demands something of you. I have noted the good manners that they elicit many times when I have visited similar palace rooms. In all instances,

Previous page: elephant at the head of a procession carrying the important insignia the fish (which must be first) and behind the lion insignia of the Maharao of Kutch.

Opposite: interior of Wankaneer Palace a typical interior of the period described here.

TEA WITH HIS HIGHNESS

29

Vijay Palace Mandir 14/9/09

the rooms with their inherently distilled atmosphere cast a spell which is conducive to courteous manners and overall promotes the art of conversation to a more thoughtful level.

With the room's stuffed seating and its small tables set around for drinks and snacks, I was happy to sit and look forward to my tea and the company of His Highness.

His Highness kindly asked about my family, in particular after my youngest son. As we talked in the quietness of the room, the elderly servant (who has spent his whole life in the Rao's service) silently came and set down delicate, white and gold-rimmed, porcelain tea cups, saucers and plates, which gently tinkled as he placed them on the marble-topped tables. He poured us tea from a silver teapot set on a silver tray, and after serving us hot, tasty snacks wrapped in crisp, flaky pastry quietly withdrew.

His Highness is a tall, slim man with a delicate, aesthetic face, a long, aquiline nose and deep, expressive Mogul eyes. He has one of the most beautiful faces I have ever seen. It is an old face in that it presents an aristocratic, historic India, which the imagination could envisage set in the chequered past of states in intrigue and at war with each other. To an artist such as myself he presented a perfect subject for a portrait.

I had come to talk about my proposed book on the village. Dhordo is a village which was settled in the Kingdom of Kutch some four hundred years ago. The original settlers, having travelled all the way from Persia, were given permission to settle in Banni by a benign maharaja of that time. It follows that I give importance to the fact of the village being enfolded within the Kingdom. The Kingdom of Kutch has played a formative and important role in the lives of the villagers. Habits and customs have been shaped, fashioned and brought into being under the rule of the maharaos.

His Highness looked over my sample project and made the following observation regarding my use of the spelling of Kutch. He thought I might consider changing my spelling which I had as "Kachachh" to what it was before Partition. He told me the history of the name and its change from Cutch to Kutch. After Partition the new Indian government did not change the name, as they did with Benares to Varansi, or Madras to Chenai, but merely changed the spelling from Kutch to the longer Kachachh.

That the government commonly used the new spelling is born out by my old government permit to visit Dhordo in 1984, which has Kutch spelt Kachachh. Now, the old, shorter version is more commonly used.

A large section of my book examines the rich embroidery produced for garments and household items by all the Banni communities. It was pertinent to discuss this with His Highness, as there

is a big change taking place in the dress of the village men and women. The men have almost completely exchanged the traditional garments for Western shirts and pants, and now the women, particularly the young women and girls, are following suit. Their individual, distinctive, richly embroidered dress is being exchanged for a more commonplace, printed, factory-made dress. It is a loss of a domestic art carried on by tradition from mother to daughter down the generations. This historic thread is now being broken. We discussed the fact that the village women now do not want to be different from their neighbour (the embroidered women's garments, designs, stitch, and style were previously distinctive to each group and village) but want to share a bigger commonality. The women all watch television, so I suggested they are seeking to be part of a modern, bigger India, rather than feel that they are presenting themselves as museum exhibits.

His Highness took the conversation another way, and expressed a different view, saying he firmly believed in a God and therefore what God directed or what changes came about would, he felt, be all acceptable. He suggested that maybe there would be other gains and ways that would be of a greater benefit, which we as mortals were not to know or perceive. He said, "You have to accept what God gives or takes away."

His Highness then talked about the loss of the tiger and the current lamentation and great publicity there is at the moment in India over this, the present head-count of the tigers in India being just some fourteen hundred. However, His Highness said that in America there are now many thousands of these same tigers, as they are being bred there, so while the tigers are in decline in India they are thriving elsewhere. Therefore, change in traditions should not be lamented. However, he considered my book would be beneficial in that it records these changes at this time.

He also felt that my book, alongside other books on similar or allied subjects, added to the understanding, knowledge, and appreciation of Kutch. His Highness requested to have a synopsis of my book.

Mochi embroidery, (made by the cobbler caste using a fine awl) made for the royal household and later developed for the European trade.

TEA WITH HIS HIGHNESS

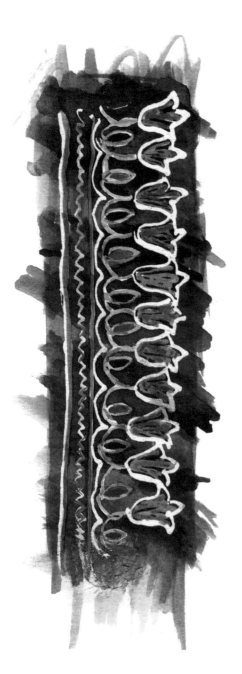

Above: border of Mochi embroidery,.
Right: an example of Mochi embroidery developed and exported for the western market.

Our cups were being silently collected when I requested a second cup of tea. I think His Highness is a man of set habits and takes only one cup of tea in the afternoon. A second cup was brought for me, which I really enjoyed. English tea is a refreshing change after a long run of chai, which one can only take in small amounts, which is why it is always served in very small cups, it being so rich, sweet and strong.

His Highness then called his secretary in order to give me some very helpful contacts regarding my book and with directions of how I should send the synopsis to him. I thanked him for his very pleasant company.

It was a most agreeable and enjoyable meeting. I was accompanied through the garden and a rickshaw was hailed for my departure by the same elderly servant.

One year later, armed with my synopsis and the first part of my book in printed form, I again went to Ranjit Vilas for tea with His Highness. His Highness was pleased to see the progress of my book and to give a dedication and it was arranged for me to come a few days later to collect this. In the end I had two further tea times with His Highness, during which he unfolded some very personal history and stories of his family.

The first occasion was when I showed him the title page of the book. He expressed pleasure that I had used the fish to illustrate the page. His Highness thought it was very auspicious, as the fish held a place of great honour in his family. In 1757 the "golden fish" (interestingly with teeth) had been given to his ancestor, Maharaja Dhiraj, by Akbar the Great Mogul. It had been presented to him by Jahangir, his son, in Ahmedabad. This honoured gift has been carried at the head of every state procession ever since.

His Highness then told me several very interesting stories and reminiscences regarding his family. Because I am an artist, he wanted to show me a portrait executed in England by Hall, a portrait painter who was commissioned by Queen Victoria in the year of her jubilee, 1887, to paint his grandfather, Maharao Khengarji. The grandfather came as a young man to the court of Queen Victoria. She took such a liking to him that she made him an aide de camp and he would always ride with her on state occasions. Queen Victoria commissioned his portrait for the gallery in Osborne House, where it is today. However, before making the life-size portrait, a portrait of twenty five percent was first made, and this is this one which is still in the royal family of Kutch's possession.

Osborne House has strong Indian associations. It houses a collection of paintings of Indian persons and scenes, painted at Queen Victoria's request. There are depictions of Indians either resident in or visiting Britain in the 19th century. Maharao Khengarji falls into the latter category, as he was visiting and an aide de camp to the queen.

In 1883 when he was just seventeen years of age he married two queens simultaneously. Both queens had their own separate palaces. This was a lively, personable young man who had come to the crown when he was only nine years old. By the time of his marriage he had been king for eight years; shortly after his marriage he came to England and to the court of Queen Victoria. After his five years with her, he gave up his post to return to India and take up ruling his Kingdom.

Certainly, the British lauded him with extra titles and His Highness pointed out to me that you had to take care to write neatly otherwise you would run out of space on an envelope. You addressed him as: Maharaja Dhiraj Mirza Maharao Savai Bahdour G.C.S.I. G.C.I.E. Khengarji the Third.

G.C.S.I. means Grand Commander of the State of India and G.C.I.E. means Grand Commander of the Indian Empire. Titles to the kings of Kutch have been bestowed through the centuries. In 1549 the title of Rao was given, and then, at the time of the gift of the fish, the title of Maharao - King of Kings - was bestowed.

His Highness then told me the following story: "I was very fond of my grandfather and as a child my grandfather visited me every day on a changing rota. Sometimes it would be at nine o'clock and sometimes at nine thirty. But, whatever the time, I looked forward to his company, as he was always good fun. It was innocent pleasure with my smiling grandfather tumbling me around and giving me his exclusive time.

"But one day I observed he was not his usual happy self, so I asked him, 'Grandfather, what is wrong?' He denied there was anything for some time but I persisted and my grandfather eventually replied, "Today I have a problem". I in my boyish way replied, "Why should you have a problem, you are the King?" He then told me his chief minister was asking him to give the death sentence to a man who had been proved guilty. I always remember my grandfather saying, "I have not the power to give life but only the power to take it away".

I responded by saying, "Then do so quickly and don't think about it any more". On that, he took up my pen and signed, but he then threw the fountain pen away: it obviously troubled him greatly to take a man's life.

In time he bought me another fountain pen. I noticed it had not got the guarantee with it. Grandfather said, "The word guarantee may be written on the front but on the reverse you will find so many rules that there is no guarantee. But as King my word is my guarantee". "And making my word my guarantee," said His Highness, "I pride myself on doing as well".

His Highness's grandfather evidently also took great pleasure in the fact that in his reign and government of sixty-six years the economy of Kutch had risen by just 25%. But after his death, in a mere six years, the economy rose by 25%.

Each state had a gun salute awarded out of 21 guns. Seventeen or 19 were the numbers of guns that saluted

Aina Mahal
The Palace has beautiful architectu

142

Threader

Kutch, but never 18 guns. If His Highness's father went to the Viceroy he would fire 31 guns for the Viceroy and 17 guns for himself, but if the Viceroy came to Kutch he would fire 31 guns for him but 19 guns for himself.

When he was a child His Highness's father would often visit Gandhi and Nehru and take his son along with him. However, if it were an official visit, his father would never request permission for him to attend; he would be left waiting outside. If it was a social visit, his father would always take the child in with him. His father was very punctilious and would never create a precedent when he was attending for an official visit. The friendship between Nehru and His Highness is apparent in the picture I was shown of His Highness as a young man shaking hands with Nehru at an official occasion.

TEA WITH HIS HIGHNESS

TEA WITH HIS HIGHNESS

Lord Krishna as a baby sitting in the lotus flower with his sheath of quivers. Lord Krishna is revered by the royal household and throughout Kutch

Baby Krishna

His Highness then told me how his father was invited to the wedding of Queen Elizabeth. His father spent a lot of time in London after Partition and was there when the Indian High Commission received just three wedding invitations and felt greatly honoured to receive one of these.

We then talked about the distinct differences of Kutch. His Highness said there were many customs and cultural aspects which were totally different in the Kingdom of Kutch from the other Indian states, which made it a place apart. Besides language and coinage - Kutch had its own mint -there was a different calendar, different marriage customs, different laws and different weights and measures and it had its own import tariffs and taxes. It differed in its time, as well, in the apparel of the court and in the many communities within the state. The music and musical instruments were also different. His Highness believes this evolved gradually over the centuries when the state was not in communication with outside states and therefore sought its own ways, its natural geography separating it for much of the year from its nearest neighbours.

We then talked about Dhordo village and His Highness's connection with it. As a young man he liked hunting, as his father had before him. His father had taken hounds from Mr Gulbeg, who bred the Kutchi version of the Sindhi hound. His Highness continued this practice and had taken as many as six dogs during his youth and up until 1970. He would be visiting a different part of Kutch and find himself without a dog to go hunting with and would send to Mr Gulbeg for a hound. The dog would be sent to him promptly. Mr Gulbeg also liked hunting, which is why he bred these dogs, and also at that time there was much game in Banni.

There is a genuine warmth and regard between His Highness and myself and I always greatly enjoy his convivial company: taking tea with him is a pleasure and precious to me. Our conversations over the tea times moved to different subjects of family, of his and mine, and I think an interesting observation with which to end this chapter will be His Highness remarking on how the circle of life goes round and comes again – "like the tying of a turban which goes round and round". Very philosophically, he then said "The only constant and permanent thing in life is change!"

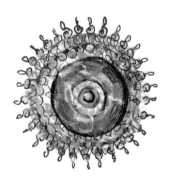

Four brides identically dressed and wearing
the nose ring particular to the Mutwa community.

Chapter 9

Village weddings

The village is in a stir, as four Mutwa weddings were being celebrated in nearby Gorivali village this day and on the following day. This evening the "Nikah", the religious wedding contract, was being conducted. At this ceremony all ladies excepting the bride are excluded, the ladies and children going to their own celebration while all the men and boys attend the Nikah. For many days the women have been sitting outside their houses plying their needles in order to finish lavish embroidery on dresses for themselves and the children.

During the day, everybody had taken a bath and made careful, extensive toilettes, the men busy trimming their beards and nails, and with much hair-combing and hairdressing for both sexes, and everyone selecting and putting on their best clothes. One after the other the children were dressed in the new embroidered garments with their hair immaculately dressed in various styles, with braids and bows and jewellery in ears and on necks and wrists. While the excited girls and boys tore about in their new glad-rags, the mothers and grandmas and all the women then donned their finery, with many, especially the older women, wearing the Mutwa traditional garments of the embroidered Kungaree top, baggy pants and embroidered head-covering. The traditional jewellery was worn by many women. This comprises the heavy silver necklace, four earrings often made of gold worn on the part top of each ear, and, very importantly, many women were wearing the Mutwa nose ring special to their community. This goes through the central part of the nose, with the jewel hanging down over the mouth. I always think it looks rather like a decorative padlock. Some ladies also wore jewellery on their foreheads, the two loops curving down to the ears from the central parting.

At about five o'clock the men began to leave from the front of the village through the reception area, into the many waiting vehicles, while we ladies and children went through the back of the compound to several jeeps. We were an exotic, glittering group of women and children. We were closely seated in the jeep, at least twelve women and children crammed together, all trying to protect newly ironed outfits and neat hairstyles.

Gorivali is a journey of about four kilometres on the sealed road and about half a kilometre across Banni. We circled the big village until we came to the Mutwa enclave, where we unpacked ourselves from the jeep and straightened our garments quickly before being enthusiastically welcomed with hugs, handshakes and namastes everywhere. I felt the strength of the Mutwa community and the kinship and the sheer joy that was so clearly expressed by everyone in seeing each other. They literally are one huge family, as everyone is related to each other. As there were several hundred people, it was clearly going to take all evening for everybody to catch up on the news and gossip.

We were ushered into one of the houses, where everyone sat on the floor and then tea was sent in. I noticed how the ladies lifted the nose jewel by holding the cup with the thumb and second finger and with the index finger lifted the nose ring in order to drink. There were not enough cups and saucers to go round so people shared the cups and saucers and we all drank enthusiastically as the chai was a very good cardamom masala.

Then a big tied-up bundle was brought in and opened: and there was the first dowry. This is what the bride would be taking with her to her marriage. There were heavy, silver anklets and rich, gold jewellery sets in cases, a wrist-watch and many other items of jewellery, and specially embroidered dowry pieces. There were ordanies and embroidered tops with the complicated Gujarat stitch (the Maltese cross already mentioned in chapter two). Gorivali has at this time several ladies who still excel at it. All four brides had very similar sets of jewellery and dowry. This was fair as all four brides are related.

It was good to see the strength of the culture. The vivid colours that all the ladies and children wore dazzled the eyes. It was a riot of colour, with one dazzling pattern upon another, and with the glitter and flash of the shisha mirrors emphasised by the humid density of the crush of people: it was overwhelming in its impression on me. In all my years in India I had never managed to attend a village wedding.

The children and the women are almost without exception very beautiful. Most have the long, classic Mogul hooked nose with the deep-lidded eyes. The darkness of the rooms cast deep shadows on their faces and garments, throwing their features into greater relief and so making them more handsome still. I drew as many faces as I could in what little time and light I had.

After examining the dowry, we went to the other three houses, which were either the new homes for the married couples or the family home of the young women. The brides were not present, as they were with their bridegrooms and with the men attending their wedding.

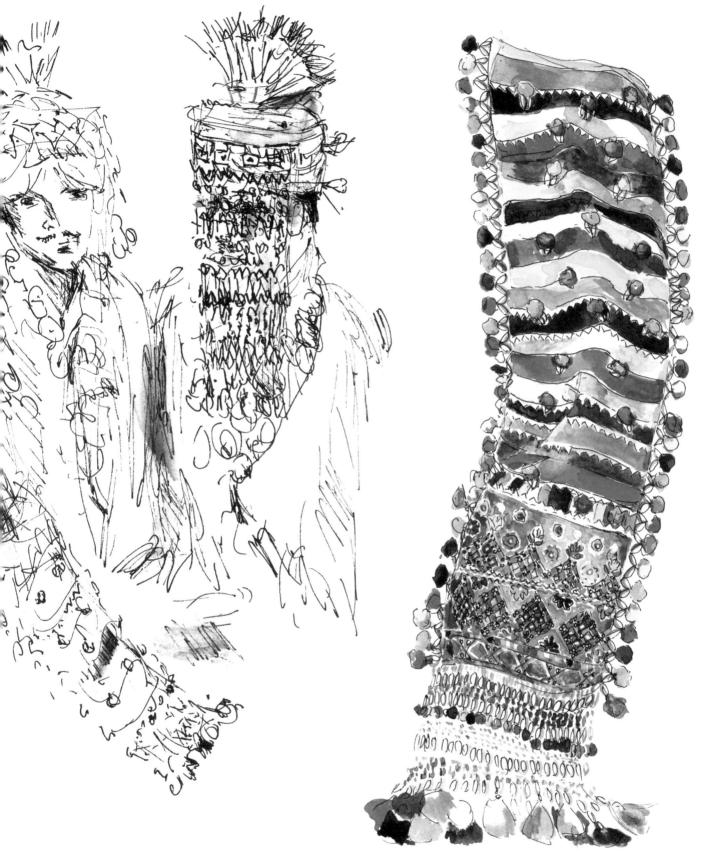

At about eight o'clock we were served food on steel plates. This was very good buffalo with the rice cooked in the juices of the meat. Often people shared a steel plate between them and more food was served as people wanted. Before the meal our hands were first washed, with water being poured over them into a brass bowl from a spouted vessel, and after the meal washed by the same method again.

Mrs Gulbeg (Mr Gulbeg's widow), who had held out well as she is in her eighties, put her feet up on one of the beds, which was a dowry gift, and her friend came to chat with her as she lay propped up on the pillows. At about 9.30 some of the children and some of the adults, including myself, went back to Dhordo in the jeep, leaving the younger ones to continue enjoying themselves.

I slept well, got up and dressed as usual, thinking that the feast to celebrate the wedding would be in the middle of the day. So I was surprised to find I was to be ready by 10.30.

As on the previous day, the men went out through the reception area while we women and girls departed from the back of the compound in the jeep of Miaw, the headman. I sat with Sifyer's sister, Tabushan, in the front with one child between us and another on Tabushan's knee. I think we were even more squeezed in than the day before. The jeep was definitely filled beyond its normal capacity, with mostly the same people but in differently brilliant costumes. The feeling was evident that this was a very special treat and a holiday. The women seldom go out of the village, so they were highly-charged and excited. Getting our sitting arrangements right made us late setting out and, as the Gulbegs are the premier family, our hosts were expectantly waiting for us.

Previous page: two bridegrooms wearing turbans and the beaded veil in which they come to the wedding (one has it thrown back).

An embroidered bag for distributing prasad (a sweet), in exchange for which money is given.

We went into the village and into the round central house, which had been cleared of fittings, to pay our respects to the brides who were seated all together on the floor. The four young women were wearing splendid, matching, gold brocade wedding dresses. Three of the four brides are sisters, with the fourth being their cousin. They were being married to two sets of first-cousin brothers.

The brides sat so closely to each other in their rigid, gold brocade outfits that they looked as though they were one body with four heads. The gold dresses were completed by the fringed, gold-fabric ordanies, the fringing standing up and framing their faces. They were a massed vision of gold, making a stunning picture, their beautiful faces set off by the traditional, gold central nose rings.

Seated to one side, but in front of them, was a woman with a book, and directly in front was a large, steel vessel containing prasad. Prasad is a sweet or sweets. Here it consisted of white, dry grains which are easily handled. One by one, each woman or girl came to give her respects and give money to the brides. Each gift was recorded in the book kept by the seated woman, and in exchange each guest was given a handful of prasad.

When this was completed, we were served a meal which was the same as last evening's but with the addition of a sweet and accompanied by a steel tumbler of buttermilk.

 We then rose and Sifyer conducted me into the central compound and a chair was found for me. In front of me were seated Sifyer and the eldest daughter of Miaw, who was equipped with a book and pencil. Standing round us clutching their presents were gathered the guests. The

Two men's marriage shoes worn in 1975. The leather has been worked with interlacing. The right shoe has washed gold on the interlacing with silver thread. Drawn 1975. The height of the right shoe's heel is interesting.

gifts being given were for the bridegroom, and again their gifts were being recorded. As each gift was passed to Sifyer she told the giver's name, what the present was and to whom it was being given, which was duly recorded. The most usual presents were ordanies, lengths of fabrics and household items.

The pile of goods got bigger and bigger. Water pots, cooking vessels, the odd clock and plates and glass sets were passed over - everything a household would need - and as there were four weddings there was an absolute mountain of goods. Therefore, to record to whom the present was given was an important task, which took up at least two hours. After this the people broke up and settled down to chatting to each other.

I have never before experienced the fraternity, companionship, friendship and love that all this community bears towards each other. I can only compare it to the love of a family for its members, except on a huge scale. The warmth and quality of love and regard is something remarkable.

The men celebrated their day with a feast in several tents set up outside the village, with several thousand men attending. As an honoured guest I could have walked out to join them but, as I was already having a more than rich, full day, I decided not to go. Moreover, I was aware there was a strong possibility of a forthcoming wedding in Dhordo.

On returning to Dhordo, we met to exchange news with the returning men. It was a mellow, quiet time and we were all well content with our day.

On the 14th March 2009, Dhordo held two weddings and hosted some 5,000 people over the two days of the weddings.

The two marriages were to be celebrated between members of the close Gulbeg family. Ali Akbar's daughter, Tabushan, and son, Hedda, were being married to a son and daughter of Ali Akbar's sister Poppeli. Marriages between first cousins are not unusual in India and in the Muslim villages of Banni. Multi marriages are usual, as it is practical and saves money. While this close custom of marriage is common, no community will intermarry with another Muslim community, and indeed they do not like marriages to take place between villages of the same community. Each of the Banni communities migrated from different countries and settled in the area over several centuries. Their dress contributes to setting each community apart and gives each its own distinction. Other Muslim communities are converted Hindus, such as the Pathan.

group of wedding guests in their finery.

Both the nose rings shown are actual size, and drawn in 1975. The top was the nose ring put on at a woman's wedding, which replaced the lower nose ring worn everyday. Now neither is worn excepting for marriage ceremonies where the smaller is worn as shown in the picture of the four brides.

Mr Gulbeg sagely told me on more than one occasion when I questioned this, "Lorna, why give God's best gift away"! The answer shows how the women are valued and appreciated for the daily work they accomplish.

I have known the young people who were being married all their lives, and they made two very handsome couples. Their new homes are within the central Gulbeg compound. Years ago, when her children were small, Poppeli started to build a row of three houses for three of her five sons. Each time she and her husband saved some money they built a little more of the three houses. Out of Poppeli's five sons, two are already married and so two houses in the row are occupied. Now the third son is being married, so the row will be complete. Luckily, her other two sons are only sixteen and twelve years old, so she has time to gradually build houses for them. Already there is discussion about where the next two houses would fit in on her compound. Her brother, Ali Akbar, the father of Hedda, has a house ready for him next to his other married son, Alladin.

When the dates for the marriages were finalized, I was away. The family had promised to telephone me to let me know when the marriages would be, but they had mislaid my number and so I was informed very late. I had just made an eighteen-hour train journey and reached my friends' house in Ahmedabad. To make another nine-hour journey was very daunting but, as I had always missed the important family weddings, I wanted to be there for these two couples whom I had known since they were born.

I took an overnight bus and arrived to find my taxi waiting to take me out to the village. We went to Prince Hotel, where I washed and changed and took a welcome breakfast. I bought some fruit and departed for the village.

My taxi pulled up beside two huge tents which had been erected outside the village for all the male guests coming from many villages and from Bhuj. I had arrived on the second day, the day of the feast. I walked into the village to find it transformed. In the open spaces between the houses frilled canopies had been strung. All the open area was now shaded with a purple and orange-frilled roof. It made it a cool area with the frills moving in the breeze and set the scene for the festivities.

Poppeli's bhunga (or round house) had been re-thatched and looked very lovely. The outside of the row of her three sons' houses had been repainted with a lilac band at the bottom and a white band above. Two sons were already married and the third empty house waiting for the newly married couple was painted inside with a cool blue. Very fresh and nice. Hedda's house had also been painted outside with a band of blue round the bottom and up the sides. His house stands alone and is an oblong shape with outside steps up to a roof terrace. The inside had been painted a creamy yellow.

The evening before had been the Nikah. The ladies had celebrated this in Miaw's compound and, as this is a more modern village, music was played. The men also had music played in one of the big tents. Because this is the most celebrated family in Banni, it made it an exceptional wedding. So many people attended that the musicians were not allowed to go, and they played and sang well into the small hours. As well as the music and dancing, photographs were allowed, but no alcohol.

I arrived mid-morning when all the guests for the feast were gathering. Ladies from outlying villages came and many stayed for a two- or three-day holiday. There was a fine group of Jat ladies whom I was able to draw over the next few days as they sat around chatting and enjoying the company of the village ladies. A wedding such as this offers many women a rare treat to leave their village and the daily grind of their lives.

Gradually the compound filled with the village women and children decked out in their jewellery and wearing rich, highly coloured, embroidered garments with the shisha mirrors in the embroideries flashing in the sun. This was even more spectacular than at Gorivali and such a bevy of women traditionally dressed I had not witnessed since 1975. At that time, the Mutwa women all wore ivory bangles in graded sizes from the wrist up the whole length of the arm. These were put on in childhood, and the arm grew to hold them. Now they are made of plastic and only the older women wear them. Many ladies were wearing new sets. It was good to see this, even if it was a facsimile.

Many different communities attended. It was not difficult to recognise the main communities as the dress is so distinct. Haliputra and the Pathan villagers, whom I know very well, were all wonderfully dressed in their long choli tops, richly embroidered with gold or silver work, at which they excel. They gave me a hearty welcome, with many hugs and handshakes.

The two brides were in family houses and each had their own dowries on display for all to see. These comprised gold jewellery, sometimes in sets, some silver items and many embroidered outfits and quilts.

Dinner was served as at Gorivali, with much the same menu, which is buffalo with the rice cooked in the meat's juices. However, I went and joined the Hindu guests, both men and women, in the vegetarian tent set up outside. It was a very good meal and nicely served with many different dishes. Many ladies had accompanied their husbands from Bhuj for this special occasion.

There was second tent for the non-vegetarians and this tent was also the tent for all the men who had come from all the other villages in Banni. I am told that the wedding attendance set a record since the time of a wedding when Mr Gulbeg was alive in 1976, when over five and a half

Marriage necklace drawn in 1975
the same design is still worn now.

158

thousand people came. This wedding drew nearly the same numbers. Among the guests were five doctors from Bhuj, the Member of Parliament for Bhuj, the District Development Officer and many more important people in an official capacity.

After dinner, I returned to the ladies to find two groups set up to receive the gifts for the husband of each couple, as in Gorivali each guest giving a gift and it being recorded in a book. The amount of goods was amazing and exceeded that at Gorivali. It is indeed enough for setting up a complete household, as it later transpired.

Another ceremony then took place where a finely embroidered bag with a long beaded fringe some eighteen inches long, traditionally a cushion piece, is used as a bag and filled with sweets (or prasad). Each husband held a bag. They came wearing the traditional Ajrakh turban and with a beaded veil over the face. Each man went round distributing the sweets and in exchange people gave them money, which they put into their turbans.

Late in the afternoon, good-byes were said and the many lorries, tempo travellers, motor bikes and buses and cars assembled outside the village went away loaded with the throng of the tired but happy marriage guests.

Marriage customs following the wedding

I awoke next morning to a village carrying out traditional wedding customs. All the wedding presents were being distributed to the two households. Big parcels in glittering wrappings, shiny tin boxes, water pots, sets of glasses and steel tumblers and tali sets began to be stacked up outside the two new but empty houses. Then, with the sorting over, the presents were carried inside.

Setting up the house was the job for some of the young girls in the household, who joyfully began to tear the wrappings off the parcels and put the contents into the cupboards in each house. Then the happy task began of putting all the dishes, glassware, steel items and glittering cups and saucers, vases of bright, artificial flowers and ornaments into arrangements on the shelf running round the top of each house. China is not stored in a cupboard as in the West; it is on display. Everyday wear is hung on hooks or in a plate rack in the communal family kitchen.

I had not before realised that this was why the shelves were created and, indeed, how the households came into being. It is not, as I thought, a gradual build-up of items, as is the tradition in the West. A new household comes into being immediately after the couple is married and is brought about entirely through wedding gifts.

The bride sits in the room and presides over the proceedings and, if she feels strongly, she will advise where an item should go; otherwise, the girls do it all. It is such a traditional arrangement

girl at wedding
— the shiney, glittering
fabrics, fringing,
beadwork and use
of rich rich braid is
favoured by all
ladies and girls.

that it needs very little direction, which I have described previously, but is good to describe further. Metal, flower-painted boxes for storage are set up in a pile. Next are two piles of quilts, which reach to the ceiling. These are all new and will have taken the whole family some considerable time to make, as they are not only quilted but will have been embroidered in the centre. Then, water pots are stored in two tall columns on either side. Finally, the small items of glasses and plates fill the top shelf.

Both the houses now look very pretty, with rich interiors created in front of my eyes.

The giving of presents also goes on for several days with visitors who were not able to attend the wedding coming from Bhuj and elsewhere to give wedding presents. Today, two doctors' families well- known to the family came with presents, besides many ladies from the Harijan community in the village. The Harijans themselves had a wedding, which is the reason they have only arrived now.

Another tradition is the many special dinners or feasts given over the next few days in each of the parents' homes and in the other immediate family houses, for the wedded couples.

I have taken away with me many happy memories. The giving and taking of love, kinship, community and identity far exceeds anything I have ever experienced at the time of a Western wedding. There is so much love and regard given to the couple at this time that the warmth bestowed on them must give the two couples a wonderful beginning to their married life. It is an experience I will never forget and I am aware that I have been very privileged to have been here at this time.

There is a security in the set rituals and culture that this community possesses, and, because of this, they are a proud and confident people. They know their history and customs and are rightly proud to be Mutwa.

Samat, the very well known Jews
harp player from Jurawada.

Chapter 10

Village music

On my first and subsequent visits I have been entertained by Dhordo village musicians and vocalists. In 1984 when my son and I visited the village, Ali Akbar, then a young man in his twenties, sang while drumming the cupboard with his fingers for the beat. He was accompanied by another musician playing the sitar. Since then, I have heard Ali Akbar sing many times, although now he chooses not to sing outside the village. There is a strong musical talent running down the generations of the Gulbeg family.

The music played is the folk songs and stories sung down the generations, keeping the village history of Banni alive. These are not the court ragas, which they also know and can play, but their own stories made into songs. The songs are delivered in a harsh voice from the throat.

This year, I was lucky enough to hear music being played on several occasions in the village. When visiting the Ajrakh khatri printer, I had met a musician from France called Fady. Fady, who is of Arab origin, was researching and recording Indian folk music for a series of programmes he planned to host in France. We talked and then parted, only to meet again unexpectedly in Dhordo.

Fady had met Alladin at the same wedding I had been invited to at the festival of Mekan Dada. I regretted that I had not attended the occasion, as there had not been one wedding but ten weddings. Both Alladin and Fady had played at the weddings, which had been celebrated for the whole night in song and music. Alladin had invited Fady to come to visit him in Dhordo. I drew Fady's attention to Ali Akbar's wonderful singing and brought Ali Akbar over to meet Fady. Ali Akbar then agreed to sing for Fady.

An impromptu concert was set up in a bhunga, with another vocalist joining Ali Akbar. Fady set up his recording equipment and I got my art materials ready. It was a very good two hours. Ali Akbar is a slight man with a finely carved, aesthetic face. Wearing his gold-embroidered Sindhi hat, he sang with passion and with dramatic gestures, his khol-ringed eyes flashing as he thrust his arm towards you, so enfolding you in the song. The second vocalist was brought in and took the song over - he was of dark visage with black hair, and his voice was rich and deep as he sang to the accompaniment of Alladin on his harmonium.

In a break between songs, Ali Akbar told of the gift of music through the generations in his family, from his grandfather, who played the long pipes, then his father, Mr Gulbeg, who also played the long pipes, now down through him and again the gift coming to his son, Alladin. Ali Akbar maintained music and singing was a rare gift coming from God, which transcended words, language barriers and differences of people, and which spoke in another voice and touched people in another way.

Alladin had many guests coming on Friday, so Fady was invited to come and play with the other musicians. Fady presented a romantic figure with his long pigtail and long, loose top and baggy pants. He is a mixture of Syrian and Algerian Arab, with pale skin, hooded eyes and fine, hooked nose. Before the afternoon ended, he got out his long pipes. Traditionally the long pipe is played with the short pipe. The long pipe makes the drone and the short pipe the tune. Fady's long pipe was decorated with a fringe of Saurashtra bead work. I would call it snake-charmer's music (the same instrument was played by the snake charmer pictured in chapter four). I can visualise the snake being mesmerised by the drone, making it sleepy, while the tune transfixes it.

But before Friday came, other guests arrived at the village and I joined them in the evening. We were seated round a camp fire eating our dinner when the musicians and singer came in and

seated themselves on the other side. The instruments were numerous: there were two which in appearance were not unlike the sitar - but with a longer length attached to the bowl - called a tambura. The tambura has three strings which are plucked and make the drone. A bell-ringer uses two small brass bells, which are struck one against the other, and then two bells on a long thread, which are twirled around with the bells striking each other and giving a long ring. A pottery water pot with a skin over the top and a steel bowl each produced different drumming sounds. Another player had pairs of metal discs set in strips of wood. He held a pair in each hand and struck one against the other, so making the discs ring. Another musician was the vocalist, and with Alladin also singing and playing his harmonium this made up the troupe of seven performers.

The sounds made by the group of instrumentalists, together with the harsh raw singing coming from the throat, is powerful and passionate. It is a music strange to me, although I have heard Ali Akbar sing in this manner. It touches a chord within me and speaks of the ancient landscape and their precarious living dependent on the vagaries of the monsoon.

The dark night, the stars above and the turbaned, dark-seated figures only revealed by the light of the fire made it a memorable evening.

Then Friday afternoon came, and with it Fady; he brought his computer with him and we watched his film of a Sindhi group recorded in Paris. They made a strong visual impact with

The simply stringed tambura, which produces the essential undertone to the village music.

their orange robes and turbans, black faces and bright orange hennaed hair and beards which closely matched their garments. Again, the same resonant, urgent voice came from the throat.

It was by then five o'clock and tea time; chai was passed round and we moved to sit in the open front-reception area. Fady got out his pipes and began to play; it was like the story of the Pied Piper: one by one the village children hearing the playing came and clustered round him to listen. By instinct, and as in school, the girls grouped themselves on one side and the boys on the other. After some time, Fady sang rather than played to them. He then sang just a phrase of the song to the children, and got them to sing it back to him. They were shy at first but then they all entered into it, each singing back to the other. Fady then took out

Raj Kana left and Hari Dosa right, two friends making music together. The picture shows how big the tambura (drone) is. Hari Dosa is the percussion: strumming both the leather covered water pot, and the tin bowl.

The percussion instrument are
a tin bowl and a leather covered water pot.

Fady playing the singora
to listening children.

another instrument called a singora. I have seen and heard this played in Swat valley in Pakistan, and have also heard it played in a palace in Udiapur. However, there are now only a handful of musicians left who can play this instrument, and only a few instruments remain; it is a rare pleasure to hear it. While it was formerly commonly played in both Sindh and Kutch, there is now just one player of the singora in Kutch.

A singora is a stringed instrument, with a hollow box to make the sound resonate. It is strung with several strings. These are of different lengths being fed into the wood in a descending, shortening order, rather like a table harp. At the side are tuning keys, turned to give the right pitch. Music is produced by both bowing and plucking the strings.

Fady has attended and listened to a lot of Rajasthan and Kutch music and while in Paris he attended concerts of both Balushistan and Sindhi music. His music is a mixture from all these sources, making the melodies from the characteristics of each tradition. I found it enchanting. I was lazy and thought I would just listen. However, he went on for so long I decided to draw him. I am glad I did as it has fixed the experience for me, and I like the drawing as it has caught the essence of him.

The group of people Fady had come to play for in the evening were people from Bombay who were from a Kutchi society. They were people looking for their roots, many never having been to Kutch, as their forefathers had left many years ago. They wanted to hear Kutchi music played while visiting their homeland.

Alladin had made the seating arrangements for the audience very well, using the village strung beds with quilts over them, arranged in rows. On the raised platform between two bhungas were seated the same group of musicians I had heard previously, plus a very well-known Jews harp player. With his craggy old face and Ajrakh turban, he presented a striking appearance. Two extra drum tabla players were added, one playing a big drum on both ends, and a tabla drummer with two drums which were placed on their rings. He spent much time tuning them with a big key and hitting the tuning knobs with a small hammer. He put hand cream onto one tabla, so that he could use the palm of his hand to make the sound as well as drumming with his fingers. The drummers were getting their pitch from Alladin on his harmonium.

First was Samat playing his iron Jews harp. I am told that, if you ring his mobile, you hear him playing, and often you are so enchanted by the music you hope he will not pick up!

The Jews harp is the instrument of the goatsherd and cattle wanderers, who pass the time by playing to themselves. Samat played several pieces, the drone changing the note and tune. It is a quiet instrument and the audience was silent to catch the soft music. Samat is recognised as a master-player and has played on the radio and to the public many times.

Next, Fady was introduced and played first a solo on his two pipes to great applause. Continuing, he first raised his pipes to bring in the drums, then the tambura, then the bells, and so on till all were playing in a frenzy of zeal. It was a mixture of melodies from Kutch and Sindh, as Fady does not have the in-depth knowledge of Kutchi music. Then the audience called for the Kutchi folk songs.

Because it is the most well-known song, the vocalists started to sing the song about the cranes coming to Banni. It refers to the cranes which come from Siberia via Afghanistan and Baluchistan to spend the winter months in Banni. The song says "Welcome to the cranes. We will not kill you. Don't keep this bird. This bird must go overseas." All the musicians came in one after the other. With the starting of the song, the crowd cheered as they knew it so well and were so carried away that they clapped in time. Then the ladies took to the floor at the side and danced the Kutchi dances, from plump matrons to young women and girls.

The menu of music we went on to hear was not the ragas of the courts but the music of the villagers, their folk songs plus religious songs or, as they say colloquially, "God songs", of both Muslim and Hindu. Music is certainly appreciated by all the villagers and is alive and well.

As midnight approached, I decided to walk back. The sky was studded with stars and my way was lit by a full moon. However, as I was passing through the gate, Mitya saw me and came to offer me a ride back to the village on his motor bike. I always think I must have reached the age for discontinuing this practice; however it seems never to be so. He drove me back slowly and steadily, and I was appreciative of the ride as I was tired and I had not realised how far we were from the village.

So ended an evening of alluring and magical music.

Manjira

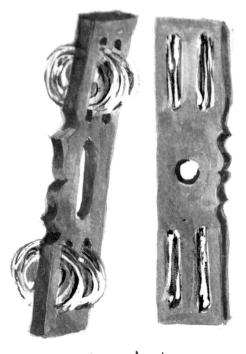

Kartal

Alladin playing his harmonium

On left are two bells (manjira) held one in each hand and clashed together continually make a harsh ringing sound. The other instrument (kartal) is one pair of two for each hand. It has circular tin discs, which make a noise when brought together. You can see the hole for the thumb and on other piece the slot for the fingers. Fingers and thumbs come together to create a continual clashing sound. On this side we have Alladin playing his harmonium.

Jat women carrying water pots.

Chapter 11

Early one morning

Miaw, Sifyer, her husband and I were sitting talking in Sifyer's house, when the subject of the price of milk came up. As the price had gone up by many rupees, it was a talking point for most of the villagers in Dhordo and the surrounding villages. The villagers' milk production is being supported and encouraged by the local government, who are subsidizing the buying of cattle and, for the poorer villager, giving him more rupees per litre for his milk.

Banni has produced abundant grass in this year of 2009, due to the last two good monsoons. The buffaloes and cows are healthy and strong, with no medicine or injections having been given. The milk can therefore be regarded as organic. In contrast to milk from the town buffalo, which has its fodder brought in, the Banni milk is considered as pure and, when mixed with the creamier cow's milk, the product is rich and excellent. The milk has now a big market as Indians have become aware of the quality of their food, so much so that, for the first time in the lives of the Mutwa, there is a break from their traditional occupation of raising cows and buffaloes to that of milk production. This is changing a tradition stretching back hundreds of years, since the Mutwa first settled in Banni. Formerly, they made ghee with the surplus milk but now they are moving into commercial milk production.

Miaw informed me that the State Bank of India was going to invest in more buffaloes for the village and surrounding villages. A collection point has been set up in Dhordo for all the surrounding villagers, where they bring their milk twice a day to be measured and a tally kept. Following this, Miaw has put in for an ATM to be installed, and, while we were talking, one of Poppeli's sons, who works for Miaw as a secretary, came in with all the subscribers' names for those opening a bank account with the State Bank of India. To set up an ATM is a truly enterprising idea, as Dhordo is so far from Bhuj.

Ingeniously, to get round the problem of accessing your account if you are illiterate, you use your thumb print. All the milk money is deposited every day into the person's account. Miaw is proposing to locate the ATM in a village bhunga, a wattle and daub house with a thatch on it,

Previous page: three Jat women: note the two first ladies heavy nose rings with the black thread supporting the weight of the ring. They are walking fast as they are all three carrying heavy containers of water and one has a child as well.

Above: Mutwa woman.

specially built for the purpose. I am not sure if he thought of this plan for aesthetic reasons but more as a bit of good humour; it will certainly come as a surprise to any stray visitor chancing upon it. How times are moving on! Sifyer observed that this was because Dhordo is now regarded as a model village. While I think this is true, I also believe it is due to Miaw Hussien's active work as a very able headman.

We then spoke of the kunj, which is a large crane coming from Siberia through Uzbekistan and Afghanistan. Miaw imitated the bird's call and asked if I had been woken up by it. As I had not, he advised me to get up at six o'clock and go out to the new tank when it is quiet and peaceful, where I would see for myself the birds descending onto the tank for water. As Miaw joked, "First they drink my water, then they go to my other hotel, the grass in Banni, and eat all the grass, so my account is zero! But I like the birds, so that is alright".

I set my alarm for six o'clock and I was out by six forty five. It was cold and dark and I looked forward to the rising sun's coming warmth. I was the only person out walking and, as I threaded my way through the village and got clear of the houses, I saw and heard hundreds and hundreds of birds twittering and calling. After some time, they flew off in great flocks, each following their leader in long, flowing lines, and I could see them descending onto Banni some distance off.

I walked up the high bank of the new tank through swirling eddies of dust stirred up by each footfall I took. My feet sank softly into the ground, giving me a sensation of treading through feathers. With the passage of people and vehicles round the village, the top soil had become loose, and, in the excavation work for the tank and the redistribution of the earth, the soil had lost all the grasses which held it together, so turning to dust. Outlines of hooves from the buffalo and cow, along with birds' feet and humans', were printed everywhere, and with each soft footstep a cloud of sweet-smelling dust arose. The swirling dust indiscernibly covers you, depositing an even grey bloom: which is why special attention is paid to covering up.

In India, harvesting the monsoon waters by collection tanks dates back to the 3rd millennium BC. The tank is built in many forms, its function being to collect the run-off from excess water and store it for later use. This age-old system is now being revived, especially in dry areas where less monsoon water is received.

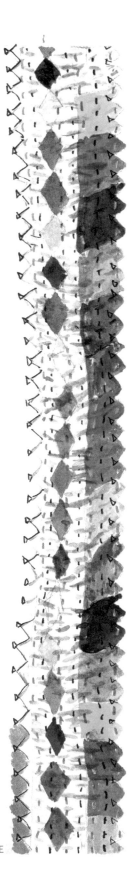

Two men walking home bathed in the light
of the setting sun.

Miaw met me on my walking back and showed me how the new tank was working. The water is first filtered and then pumped up into the water tower by the use of a solar panel and then pumped to the houses. It also goes into a concrete tank, from where the women take water to wash clothes. Miaw went to the control room below the tower and switched on the pump. He showed me the second tank, which was the original tank for the village, which he now reserves for the buffalo. This had no visible water but had a concrete trough set in the middle, in which a pipe lay. On lifting this up, water came gushing out.

At the times when there is a good monsoon, the tank will be full to the brim. Moreover, when the tank is receiving water, it will be soaking into the ground directly beneath the tank, where it stays. Gradually, with use, the visible tank water goes down until only the sandy bottom of the tank can be seen. In the centre of the tank is a pump, which then pumps up the water from below the tank. This is what I was seeing.

Miaw and I then walked back into his compound, where he first gave me a cup of chai and then some breakfast made by his wife. It was a very tasty concoction of vermicelli cooked into a sweet dish with buffalo milk. Miaw asked me, if I had time, whether I would like to see the new reserve tank he is now having built for Dhordo some little distance from the village. Yes, of course I would. So we got into his jeep and set off.

Early one morning, what could be a greater delight than going across Banni? The sweet smell of the Banni dust rose like an old fragrant memory, and I was once again back with Shri Gulberg, Miaw's father, crossing Banni. It was the same remembrance. We had left the road and were crossing Banni as before on the old tracks, the fresh smell of the land in the early morning, the sun just risen giving out a little warmth, the expanse of the land, the wide blue sky and the tufted grassland all combining to make it Banni. It felt to me that there was no other place where I would rather be.

Here, the dreaded acacia had not got a hold, so it was the old, familiar landscape. I gasped as we came to the new tank, which had just been constructed. It is not so deep but it is vast. It is stepped on two levels with packed walls of earth, but not cemented in as are the two tanks in Dhordo. It has the low point at each end for the water to enter and for the surplus water to exit by. Miaw explained that it is not excavated to such a low level as its purpose is to serve as an extra tank for Dhordo and to encourage the wild life back. I think it is a very good idea, but I was not sure how the water would stay on the surface for the wildlife. Miaw then asked if I would like to see another. Yes, of course I would. We went a little distance and found a small tank which was filled with water. Miaw knew the exact time that the birds came down to drink from this tank. It was nine o'clock, and we were much too early to see them.

I was then told that there was another very large tank being built which would supply water for a head of two thousand cattle and for the some two hundred people who make up Bitira. These Jat people have to leave their village and migrate with their cattle to find water in another part of Banni. This is called Puko. I have seen camps of Jat before on Banni. They take temporary housing with them made of cane. The cane is tied together in lengths, making walls which fold

Washing drying on the acacia tree. Here we see scarves in a typical design now commonly worn by men, replacing the former ajrakh.

together when not staked in the ground. The Jat set these in an oblong, leaving an opening for a door, and cover it with a big cloth, so forming the roof. They carry the tents and the household pots and bedding on the backs of camels.

Bitira is some eleven kilometres away from where we were, and Miaw asked if I would like to see this tank as well. On this pearl of a morning, why would I refuse? This was a good track and Miaw is not a slow driver. He went straight into top gear and the jeep sped over the sandy track. As we came to the bends, I found that I was bracing my feet against the floor, with my back against the seat to take the curves as they came flashing up, and wondered if this was not just a little too exciting! I did not think it my place to ask him to slow down - and we arrived safely.

We drove down onto the floor of an enormous tank. Its walls were lined with broken stone, and some parts were already cement-rendered. Yellow plastic containers utilized as buckets from some previous purpose now held water which was being systematically poured down the walls to halt the drying process from the sun's rays. I was truly amazed by the scale of the tank and also that several of them were being built. I was now told that Miaw was in charge of fifteen new tanks that were under construction in various villages.

I remembered the previous year when Miaw had shown me a video that he had taken at the time of monsoon, with himself knee-deep in flooding monsoon water which was too excessive for the village's original tank to cope with. Armed with this video, he had convinced the DDO that there was enough water at the time of the monsoon but that the village needed another and bigger tank in order to collect and store the water.

The video convinced the powers-that-be, and the first big tank at Dhordo was constructed. It is estimated that it now holds enough water for two years' use for the village. Further investigation showed that the monsoon water seeps into the ground and gently flows on a westwards gradient to where the Rann absorbs it. Therefore, this is a big attempt to capture the water for the Banni villages. I hope it works and think mainly it will. My reservations are that I have been in Banni on many occasions and, during my first visit in 1975, it was a time of great hardship for all the Banni villages, as the monsoon had failed completely, not just for one year but for seven years. It was such a hard time for all these remote villagers that, for the first time, they were willing to sell their embroideries.

It was then that the famine programme was put in place, which is the same plan that was designed by the British. It is still much the same today. Men and women are given work breaking stone for new roads and digging the earth out to make the roads. The earth is pegged out in sections and dug to a certain depth, for which so many rupees are paid and a daily ration of flour

Interior of Banni house.

Mulban sewing outside her house

is given. As you travel to the remote villages on these unsurfaced roads, which are built high with the banked-up earth, you can see the dug-out squares on either side. These roads suddenly terminate and you have to descend onto Banni to complete your journey. The road is quietly waiting for the next failed monsoon for its completion.

I have to add that the monsoon also failed for two years after the last great earthquake in 2001. Many cattle died and those remaining were taken to holding-pens outside Bhuj, where they were fed and watered. It will be a testing time if and when the next monsoon fails. It is, as many a villager will say, "all in the hands of God." Banni people are very devout - they live close to the earth and their very lives depend on the vagaries of the weather. There is also the fear of earthquakes, as Bhuj is built on a fault line.

However, coming back to the present, I now understand why the State Bank of India is giving development money to buy cows and buffaloes for the area, and why an ATM is to be installed for the villagers. The programme of building numerous tanks to serve the villagers in Banni, thereby ensuring water for the buffaloes and milk production, is seen by the bank as a good business and investment enterprise. It is convinced of the benefits of storing monsoon water, thereby yielding a robust milk production from the herds of cows and buffaloes. While I wish the scheme to prosper, I am concerned about the very fragile nature and foundation of this enterprise. The monsoon is fickle in this area. Sometimes the rain never falls in a year and at other times it can flood, each catastrophe bringing distress to these people. I wish the initiative every success but realize that, until there is a stable supply of water, this enterprise could easily fail.

The hope must be that, in the longer term, the project which is now under construction for bringing diverted river water from Saurashtran into Kutch will have some of the water designated and channelled into Banni. This, and only this, will redress the starvation of water from its original river sources to this area. Now, the area is totally reliant on the monsoon, whereas previously there was river water emptying into Banni. A constant flow of water will return Banni to the abundant grasslands it had in Shri Gulbeg's youth. To once again have the long grass which one had to wade through and could cut and thatch the houses with will also raise enough buffalo and milk to satisfy a growing India, and bring a renewed prosperity to the people.

At the moment, this ten-year project is being debated by the politicians, who are deciding where and to whom the water will go. For the security of the lives and employment of the Banni people, it is the one and only real answer. Meanwhile, I wish the present project every success.

Miaw and I drove back, following the undulating flight line of a great flock of cranes. So numerous were they that the single line of birds stretched almost as far as the eye could see. Lazily and gracefully they dipped and swooped on the thermals. It was as though they were on an invisible fairground big dipper in the sky, the birds rising and falling in a magnificent, waving motion.

Set against the enormous, domed expanse of blue sky, the birds threaded back for miles, keeping us company over the flat, khaki land on our return to the village. While we travelled below the flying escort, our lone jeep with its curving trail of dust created arabesques on the empty landscape: making a perfect reflected mirror image of the kunj above. And leaving me with an imprint of an unforgettable morning.

Ann reading his lesson

Chapter 12

A day in the village

The soft early dawn light barely lit my steps as, swathed in my blanket, I again made an early morning pilgrimage to catch the cranes drinking at the village tank.

It was exhilarating to be out early in the chill air, my steps crunching through the thin crust formed by the dew on the earth. The cranes were not in the tank: they had already departed and were flying in low loops about half a mile away. In their place, I was happy to watch the small waders with their long, jointed legs delicately stepping in the shallow tank water.

I strolled back to the village and met Nanima, who invited me for chai. Nanima is always up early milking her buffalo and, when I met her, had been delivering a pail of milk. I followed her to her compound and sat outside her house, watching the antics of a newly-born black and white goat. It was capering about, leaping at walls and falling down on its unsteady legs, sometimes succeeding in gaining the top of the low mud wall, only to promptly lose its balance, and once more fall off. The goat was also trying out its taste buds, and its soft little lips nibbled at everything, including my fingers and my paint brushes. It frisked about, its tiny, horned feet beating out a tap dance on the sun-baked mud of the compound platform.

I was drinking my hot masala chai when a gushing noise announced it was seven o'clock. Time for the day's allocation of rationed Government water. The water flowed into a large, plastic container, and Nanima set about filling buckets of water and emptying them into storage containers as fast as she could. The clank of the handles on the metal pails as they were set down, punctuated by the crowing of a magnificent, strutting rooster, and the ringing of the bells of buffaloes and goats, provided a melodious and constant rhythm of sound in the early morning. Backlighting this scene was the rosy glow of the sun as it began to fill the sky over the roof of the mosque.

As each buffalo came to be milked, a bag of food was looped by a rope over its head, hanging by its tight curled horns. With the animal's two back legs hobbled, Nanima began to massage the milk down the teats. When the milk came, she placed a pot on her knee and the milk hissed into it. After milking, the buffaloes were released to wander off and forage for themselves, while tethered young buffaloes and goats had bowls of food set in front of them.

The various sounds that each animal's different-sized bell made as they moved and snuffled and nuzzled their food, together with the tinkling of the little goat's bell as it practised its jumps, continued the morning's melodies; and altogether was as good a start to any day I can think of.

After the goats had been fed and milked and the food eaten by the young buffaloes, they were released and wandered off for their day's amusement, and a silence settled over the compound.

With my painting subjects having left and it now being 8.15, I decided to go to the school and sit in on the lessons, and draw some of the children. The school starts very early, at about seven thirty, and the children all had their heads down over their books when I arrived. Adding my shoes to the pile outside the schoolhouse door, I went to the front of the class, where the teacher brought me a chair to sit on, draping it with his Ajrakh turban.

The girls sit on one side, and the boys on the other. Both boys and girls wear bright clothes, the girls in salwar chemise, with colourful ordanies over their heads, while the boys wear long shirts over baggy trousers, and have patterned scarves or turbans wound round their heads. The children present an exotic picture, as though stepping out from an animated painting. The light only coming from the door deepens the colours, painting them from black to the brightest hues. This brilliance of graded colours set against a dark background, with the highlighted, tawny-skinned, black-eyed faces of the children in their pretty array gazing out at you, creates a Rembrandt everywhere you look.

I find it a rewarding challenge to draw the children: they are reluctant subjects and when they see you drawing them move shyly away. You have to observe and draw quickly and accurately.

Nine o'clock recess soon came and the children went home for breakfast. Presently, a small girl came into the empty schoolroom bearing two cups of chai for us. She made a pretty waitress with her orange scarf floating around her. As is the village fashion, the teacher cooled his tea by pouring it into his saucer, enjoying it in noisy slurps.

Class recommenced and the children began to recite out loud from their Korans. This is much the same practice as when I as a child learnt Christian prayers, such as the Lord's Prayer. I also clearly remember learning poetry and my times-tables, when the whole class would recite together. The difference here is that the children chant the text individually, while rocking to and fro. Maybe the movement helps them remember the text. Whatever it is, it creates a sea of moving sound and sight.

Pupils came one-by-one to be tested by the teacher, both sitting on the floor on either side of a low desk. With the Koran set on the desk, the pupil reads his portion with corrections from the teacher. If the child is lack-a-daisy, the teacher sometimes cuffs him on the side of the head, or gets a short switch and thwacks the side of the desk. I notice it is the boys who get this treatment; the girls all seem more dedicated to their studies.

As in British schools, the teacher calls the register, and similarly the children learn poems and songs by heart and learn to sing together, but here largely the similarity ends.

In Dhordo, the school is bare, except for a few visual aids kept in a cupboard, with nothing adorning the walls. The furniture is minimal, with low, long desks for the children and mats to sit at them. In contrast, the English primary school may well have an aquarium, posters and visual aids decorating every wall and many toys which the education system sees as aids to the children's learning. The children will have small replicas of their mother's kitchen, or prams and cots with dolls. Here in the village, the children are already helping in the kitchen, rolling the chapattis, getting well-water and milk, and carrying the babies and their small siblings around for their mother. Western educational toys would be superfluous in the village, as the children are not rehearsing for a future life - they are already living the reality.

Pails left dry.

Eleven o'clock came, and school was at an end. The pupils stood up, put their mats and desks into neat piles by the walls and skipped away through the door.

The girl who brought the teacher and myself chai wanted to take me to her house. She led me through another part of the village by a very twisting route until she came to her home, then to another family house, and finally through a passageway to her family's shop. The shop was a real surprise because I knew it from 1975; it was not the same but a new and bigger version of it. I recognised it instantly, however, from the huge set of very old scales proudly displayed and used as before. It is good to know that this shop has flourished. I requested a chair and sat and drew the scales and shop.

I visited the shop several times during my stay, as it forms a meeting-place for men to sit and chat, and I very much enjoyed observing and drawing this convivial scene.

On returning to my house, I found a small gathering of ladies round Sifyer's old house, which is next to the new one in which I stay. In the centre was the lady for whom I had bought a sewing machine at the time of the earthquake to help her make a living. She had been married and living in Bhuj, but on the death of her husband she asked the headman for permission to return to her village. It seems she makes a little living by travelling to Bhuj, purchasing small items and peddling them round the village. The women of Dhordo do not go to Bhuj, because of the purdah they choose to impose on themselves. Because the custom is different in Bhuj, where this lady previously lived, it is accepted that she travels freely. In Dhordo, the men do all the shopping for the ladies. When they were children, the girls went to school and played outside the central village compound, but, once grown up and married, they elect not to go out even to the reception area. When the rickshaw man selling vegetables comes to the front of the reception, they will request the Hindu Harijan lady who sweeps for them to purchase the items they want.

It has been noted that some of the men have very good taste. It is they who buy all the embroidery materials and threads for the ladies. However, they also buy nylon fabric for quilts and tops, which is harder

Paddle for churning butter.
Pestle for pounding medicines
for the animals

Mrs Gulbeg salvaging the webbing from her bed
which is being restrung by her Grandson.

to embroider but in the ladies' eyes it has the redeeming feature of being "easy-care".

The pedlar lady knows what the women's and children's tastes are and brings fancy, glittering lengths of ribbon to dress their head coverings, and je-jaws such as the glass bowl sets which young ladies like to gather for their dowries, or decorated plastic containers which the children put small treasures in, and other trifles. It was a chattering, excited bunch of ladies, examining and turning over the spread-out, glittering objects. The choice being made, terms were recorded in an account book and the ladies departed with their trophies.

Mrs Gulbeg, the widow of Mr Gulbeg, was sitting sewing in her usual position, warming her old bones in the sun. I sat beside her and we talked and drank tea. She is the village matriarch and has everyone's great respect both here and in all the Banni villages. As the wife of Mr Gulbeg, she was always by his side, cooking and being the hostess to his many friends, headmen from other villages, and government officials who made up a constant stream of visitors. A widow for many years, when she was eighty just six years ago, she earned even greater admiration as she left the village and went by herself on Hajj. This is the biggest pilgrimage in the world. It is regarded as a duty by every Muslim to go once in a lifetime to Mecca in Saudi Arabia.

The pilgrimage occurs from the 8th to the 12th day of Dhu al-Hijah, the 12th and last month of the Islamic calendar. The Islamic calendar is a lunar calendar and is eleven days shorter than the Gregorian calendar. Hajj is associated with the prophet Muhammad from the 7th century, but the ritual of pilgrimage to Mecca is considered by Muslims to stretch back thousands of years to the time of Abraham. Pilgrims perform a series of rituals, the main one being to walk counter clock-wise seven times around the Kaaba, the cube-shaped building which acts as the direction of prayer world-wide.

For a woman of Mrs Gulbeg's age, particularly bearing in mind that she will seldom have left the village, let alone gone on an air flight, it was an extraordinary undertaking. Now, many villagers have followed her wonderful example, but they have all gone in groups, unlike her.

In 1975, Mrs Gulbeg was a fine-looking woman in her Mutwa dress. She had all five gold earrings worn round the tops of her ears, her hair was rolled under round her head from her central parting, her tie-dyed ordani with a fine stitched border covering her head. She had bangles from her wrist to her armpit, and wore one of her own finely-worked, embroidered tops together with a full black skirt.

She was a handsome headman's wife. Mr Gulbeg was proud of her and loved her dearly. He always liked to tell you about how he took her from her village. She was of the same Mutwa community, but from the neighbouring village of Gorivali. Mr Gulbeg had seen and liked her but her parents were unwilling. The couple courted each other but neither set of parents was happy. In the end, Mr Gulbeg arranged the wedding without consent and took her from her village. By this time, she was well into her thirties, so she had her three children very late: first Poppeli, then Ali Akbar, the doctor, and then the youngest, Miaw Hussein, the present headman.

Mrs Gulbeg is now without her jewellery, as she has taken the earrings and necklace off as a sign of widowhood. This practice is copied from the Hindu custom. She has hennaed grey hair and wears very big pebble glasses tied with a string cord round her head. I wanted to give her new glasses, as her old ones are scratched and the glass is opaque through usage, but she clings to her old ones. She can no longer see to execute the fine work she used to do, but, with the bigger needles I bring her, she can do the running stitch which binds the surfaces of the quilts together.

Mrs Gulbeg has an aura of serenity. Her daughter, Poppeli, who lives next door, brings her meals to her and says quite simply, "I love my mother." As I do. She is always pleased to see me and we give each other a very warm embrace.

I could see that Sifyer's group was still occupied with buying their items from the pedlar so I decided to go to Poppeli's compound and use the computer, which is in one of her sons' houses.

girls sit on the left in school
while the boys sit on the right.

While I was checking my mail, Poppeli brought me a sweet her daughter had made, and then before I had completed my correspondence my dinner was brought in. I returned to Sifyer's house to find another dinner on the table. But the problem was unexpectedly resolved. As I turned in response to the children's loud exclamations, I found a goat with his mouth full of my chapattis making his exit from the bhunga. We all laughed as the goat got smacked on the rump but happily went off with his mouth full.

I decided to paint the Ahir blouse that my friend Jadevi (a merchant in village embroideries) had lent me, and, as I could not get a model for it, I stuffed the two breasts with my scarf, to the titters and hand-over-the-mouth laughter of the children. I displayed it on the white back of a quilt. I worked until the light began to fade and found, from the evidence of my line of cups, that while sitting there I had been served chai four times.

It was five o'clock, so I packed up and went for my evening walk, stopping on the road where a break in the trees permits the setting sun to be seen. As I stood watching, an elderly villager, who makes the most beautiful models of dogs, horses, camels, buffalo and cows from the earth of Banni, was walking down the road towards me. He very much wanted to chat to me about a project dear to his heart.

I am trying to organise a way for him to make his models in proper clay and to have them fired in a kiln. He can then sell these charming items and provide a small income for himself: it will be a good outlet for his talent. To enable him to do so, I have to arrange for him to visit the potters in Khavda. I know they will help, as they became good friends after their pottery was destroyed in the earthquake of 2001. Shortly after the earthquake, I was able to fund them for the rebuilding of their studio.

When the pottery artist first showed me these animals, he demonstrated his talent by pulling his turban down over his face and making one item blindfold. Now he chatted away to me - under the impression that I understood every word. I parted from him to continue my walk and, when I turned to look back, I saw him on his knees at the road-side saying his prayers under the setting sun.

When the earthquake of 2001 happened, I had left Dhordo with a group of tourists just two days earlier. The date was 26th January - Independence Day. It was a massive earthquake, causing great loss of life, with Bhuj being the epicentre. My group had just reached our hotel in Udaipur when we were told the news, and we watched the live broadcasts on television. We were all very upset as we were aware that many of the people we had just visited were in the path of the earthquake.

We discussed the disaster and I decided when our journey was over I would go to Bhuj to report back to my group. I would also contact all the other people I had taken to India over the last ten years and see what help we could offer, and for whom. Ultimately, I would, with the groups' support, collect funds for the artists and craftsmen in Banni. Application for the fund was advertised in Bhuj's local paper and forms were left for collection and completion with the curator of the museum in Bhuj. With the help of various headmen, the funds were dispersed. And that is how I came to fund the potters.

 On one of my visits to the potters, I found that Dhordo's infant school had come down in the earthquake. I therefore gave the remaining money to the village to start building a new school. The school came into being through stages. It is the biggest bhunga it is possible to build, being controlled in size by the span of wood needed to cross the building and support the roof.

First, the building with the traditional thatch was made, and then more money collected for the carved entrance doors and the built-in cupboard. The school was now working but needed an electricity connection for lights and fan. I finally collected enough money not only for this but also for low rows of desks and long mats for the children to sit on, and for the concrete compound and the enclosing wall. The school is next to the mosque, in the front of the village by the reception building.

The school has been a great success and is also used for village meetings when needed. It is a pleasure to visit the school and its pupils, which number up to thirty five. The children recite and sing very happily to any visitors to their school.

I was once at the school when the teacher had been delayed for over an hour. The children swept out the school and compound, laid out the mats and desks, lined up outside, sang a sweet song, entered, and were working when their teacher arrived. The teacher is a good man, who comes everyday on his bicycle from nearby Gorivali village.

Leaving the pottery artist at his prayers, I walked on, knowing by the buffaloes meandering towards me that I should return soon, as dusk was falling. The buffaloes took my mind back to 1975, when the herds would be accompanied by their herdsman, announcing their approach by the rising cloud of drifting dust and the melodies of the many animals' bells ringing as they progressed in slow fashion home.

At that time, after the monsoon, the grass round the village was first cropped. When this was over, the herdsman, taking basic items in a swag bag on a stick over his shoulder, in the manner of Dick Wittington, would migrate. Following the grass, he gradually progressed with the herds into the interior of Banni, returning at longer and longer intervals as he journeyed further and further from the village. The animals were then raised only as stock, and not for milk production, although some milk to sustain the herdsman would be taken from the mothers with calves.

Now, with the depletion of the grass, the Mutwa do not raise stock but keep milking-herds, so you will still see the animals wending their way home, coming back to be fed and milked, but without the herdsman.

As I bent my way homeward, the setting sun cast a final dash of vermilion over the village. The glow lit not only the houses but the women moving about preparing the evening meal. Fragrant wood-smoke began to filter through the grass roofs of the kitchens as the women lit their fires. Many women in the same household, each in her own kitchen, will be making a dish to contribute to the household's communal meal. Sifyer, in her household, always makes the chapattis. I found her on my return sitting by her doorway kneading the dough for the many chapattis she makes each day for her husband's family, of which she is a part. She divides the dough into small portions, and Nafisa, Sifyer's seven year-old daughter, helps her roll them out, while Sifyer, a modern woman, cooks them over her primus.

Nowadays, the chapatti is made with husked wheat flour but in 1975 the chapatti was made only from millet. This made a heavy but hearty staple and, served as it was with a blob of buffalo butter, it was filling, delicious, and full of nutrition. It is occasionally still made in this way but is not a staple. A typical meal in 1975 was composed of millet chapattis, meat curry, a vegetable curry and some jaggery (solid cane sugar). This would be accompanied by a glass of buttermilk, a simple but healthy meal.

It was the pride of the village in 1975 that if a man died at the age of 85 then he died young. Now, people die much earlier: this longevity is no longer the norm. The alteration in the diet may be in part responsible for this. Polished rice and dhal is now cooked with a few vegetables in a solid, lumpy dish which they call subji. Chapattis are made from polished wheat and there is less or none of the fresh butter to go with them, and an inferior oil is used for cooking where before only ghee was used. Meat is only now served occasionally and in small amounts, as are the vegetables, resulting in an overall lack of minerals and protein. The depleted diet has caused a marked change for the worse in the condition of people's teeth. Snacks and sweets are now also available for the children, whereas there was a total absence of these in 1975, and these too make inroads into the tooth enamel. Formerly, it was a simpler but very wholesome diet.

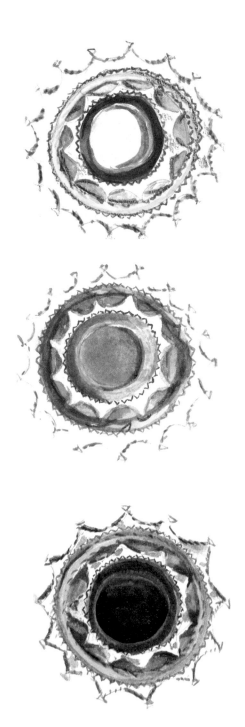

large shishas copied from a mane belt.

B

There was also less stress, as the daily round took place in or around the village. Now the men have to leave the village, and most work at the factory built about twenty years ago on the edge of Banni and the Rann, some eight miles away. Abandonment of the traditional dress of the village men was instigated by the factory, which demanded that the workers should be dressed in shirts and pants. The difference in the lifestyle of the men who leave the village on a daily basis is a tremendous change. I remember in 1975 that Mr Gulbeg said that a Jat woman would often never leave her village in Banni, and the men very rarely, and that, if they went to Bhuj, it took eight days by camel from some villages in the middle of Banni. With many villages now having sealed, surfaced roads providing access , vehicles can easily reach each and every village.

My house is never without people coming in to chat, especially in the evening. This evening, the doctor, Ali Akbar, is sitting on my bed when Miaw Hussein comes in, with his woolly hat awry on his head. Immediately, Sifyer, his niece, slides from her chair onto the floor in respect, and her father, Ali Akbar, stands up. In India this is known as giving and showing respect: to sit below or stand above are both ways of giving respect.

As headman to this village and several more, Miaw Hussein works unstintingly, and in this duty has given the villages many benefits, either from his own pocket or by pursuing their interests with the District Development Officer. So, in the villagers' and in his family's eyes, he has earned great respect, and they show it in their good manners towards him.

Two of Miaw Hussein's sons came in and stood near their father, who was by then lying on my bed. His youngest son, a truly beautiful boy of four years, is graced with the most luxuriant, long, curly eyelashes. I would love to draw him, but he is very shy and will not stay in a pose long enough for me to capture him.

I had a packet of dates, and we passed these around as we discussed some village projects. My evening dinner had been forgotten and at 10.30 after everybody had left I had some cold chapattis and a very highly spiced, gristly meat curry. When the tears ran down my face, I decided to abandon the meal and resorted to bananas and biscuits, and went to bed. I had to get up early again the next morning in order to prepare my room for some important Government visitors

: traditional way of stoulering quilts.

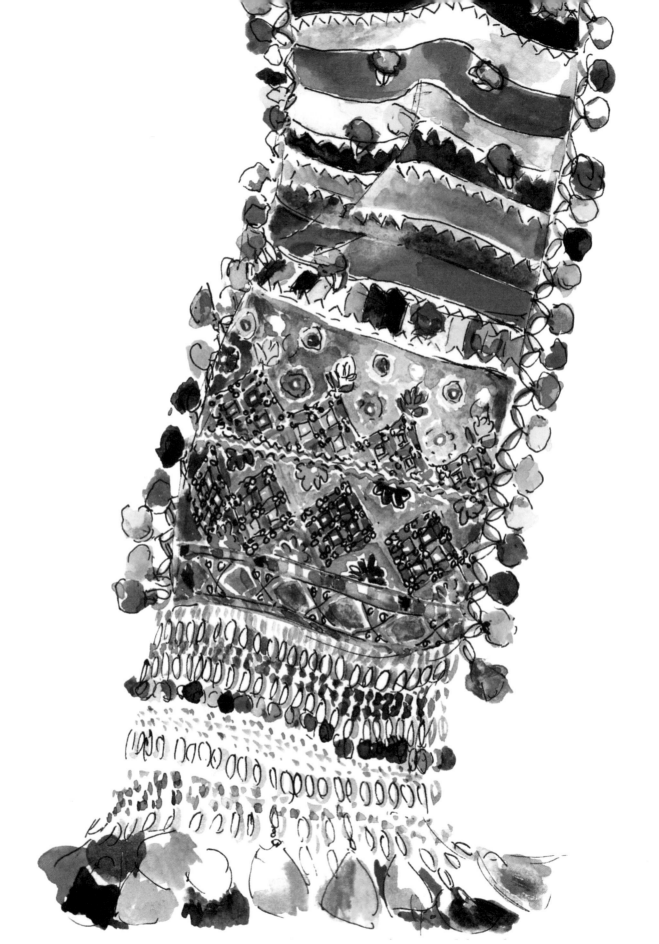

Chapter 13

Pilgrims and diary recollections

The front porch of the village reception building has always been a place of waiting, certainly since my first visit in 1975. People then walked from their village to consult Shri Gulbeg, the headman. Since the early 1980's, when Ali Akbar completed his training in medicine, people have waited for him, too.

Ali Akbar is trained in basic medicine, rather like an auxiliary nurse. When he started his work in the early eighties, there were still no roads to the village, and people walked for miles to consult him. He was the only medical person they had recourse to without the long and difficult journey to Bhuj. If patients had walked for days to attend, they would be offered the hospitality of a bed and food for the night in the reception room. Severe cases would be taken to Bhuj by private jeep or by the milk lorry, which called periodically to collect the surplus milk. Now, only a few people have to walk, his patients coming either by bus or motorbike, or by hitching a lift with a vehicle coming to the village.

I like to sit in the reception area and observe the people coming to Dhordo. Villagers come from all over Banni, together with official visitors dressed in city clothes, so that you see a great variety of dress and characters, making it a hub of interest.

For visiting his patients, Ali Akbar uses a motor bike. When I first saw it in the eighties, it was a small two-stroke bike; now it is a large, powerful one. The same Red Cross flag is on the front, and Ali Akbar carries a plastic bag, now cracked and stiff with age, to hold his medicines and stethoscope. Now as then, the women are modest, and he examines them fully-clothed and injections are administered straight through their garments.

During my long stay in Dhordo over January, February and March in 2009, I found to my astonishment that beggars visited the village, and two in particular did so on a regular basis. At first I did not recognise them as beggars; they appeared outside my door, just standing there. I looked at them for distinguishing marks of costume to identify them, but found none. I had already seen this mother, and daughter of about seven years, at the four weddings in Gorivali

The village sweet shop.

village. Seemingly, they make a round of the Banni villages, appearing in Dhordo about every six weeks, where they are always treated very generously.

On another occasion, I found a very sad-looking old man on the front porch of the reception and drew him. I gave him some rupees for his trouble and, a while after I had finished, he slowly walked away. I was told he was from a nearby village, a widower, who had also lost his children, and was on his own without money. From time to time he walks from one village to another, and everyone gives him food. It is a revered tradition in Banni that no seeker who comes to the door will be sent away empty-handed.

Over the months, I have been aware that, as I am sitting drawing, children often cluster around me, and I hear them chewing and loudly crunching sweets and snacks. Eventually I discovered where they purchase these from. When I visited Nanima's compound and went into her house, I saw, standing on a rough cupboard, plastic jars containing snacks and sweets. Children came in one by one clutching a few rupees, and bought sweets at one rupee each or for a couple of rupees a packet of puffy, crunchy items.

One day Firman, Nanima's nephew of nine months, was brought over and Nanima assembled a wooden cradle such as I saw in 1975 but now seldom see. Into this went the baby, and he sat and was rocked by another nephew. I drew the baby in the cot and then did a drawing of the sweet shop, which

A sad widower looking very lonely as he walks away.

205

Ali Akbar the local auxiliary doctor
wrapped up against the dust before
setting out to see his patients.

comprises just the crude dresser with the jars. Nanima commenced her simple embroidery work (she was edging a quilt), and I drew her as well.

We were interrupted by the mullah from Dhordo's mosque coughing his microphone into life and announcing the call for prayer. Nanima rolled out her blue and red prayer mat across the room from me, and began to pray, facing Mecca.

The Adhan's daily five calls from the mosque punctuate the village day. The first is at the break of day – calling Allahu Akbar – God is Greatest. The person chosen for reciting the Adhan is chosen primarily for his eloquent voice in making the calls clearly and beautifully. Each lady will halt her work and pay attention to her prayers. This peaceful gap of prayer is a palpable living breath in the life of the village.

Diary notes 25/2/09

I needed to have a few days in Bhuj and decided to take the early morning bus which starts from Dhordo at 7.45. In the grey light of the early morning, I walked out of the village through the reception and asked the few people gathered by the roadside where the bus arrived. I was directed to the small, concrete kiosk which acts as shop, and sat down on its steps to wait. I was one of just two passengers.

It is the custom on these village buses for the men and women to sit separately, so I sat on the ladies' side. We stopped at frequent intervals picking up passengers, and it was a real pleasure to see the brightly-clothed women from all the communities getting on and sitting around me. Several said hello, as they had met me at one or another wedding, and one of the Harijan ladies whom I had painted recognized me and was so pleased to see me that she kept turning round to smile.

As said before, most Muslim and Hindu women will not have gone beyond two kilometres from their village but - on the rare occasion when they do go outside their village - they always travel with their menfolk and walk behind them with a bowed, covered head. They will say, "We do not wear purdah but we jealously guard our honour; we veil not just our eyes but our hearts." All the village women, both Muslim and Hindu, will cover their faces when outside their village and, if an unknown man should enter their village, they will quickly pull their head covering over their faces. This purdah is their custom, and on the bus the women covered their heads and faces

The bus contained many people wearing their traditional costume, or part of it, and it is the nearest one can get now to seeing the costumes from this area. The garments have not the rich embroidery of 1975 but I recommend it as a journey if one wishes to see the remnants of this past glory.

We stopped at Birendira for the driver and some male passengers to have tea before continuing the long journey to Bhuj. Birendira is another place where I would recommend a halt to sit in the shacks which serve tea and drinks. Birendira reminds me of a cowboy frontier town, as it is such a temporary place, with its long line of ramshackle buildings on each side of the road.

Buses, lorries, and cars all halt for a break, so that it becomes a meeting place and transit stop for the villages and for Khavda, the last town next to the Rann and Pakistan. People stop for a gossip and to exchange news. Again, it is the menfolk who will mostly be seen here. The women will wait on the bus or in the vehicle, except for those who get off to walk to their home in Birendira village. The village is split into several parts, each with a different community. If you take the time, you can discern which community each woman belongs to by her garments. Sitting and observing this passing scene can be very rewarding.

Nomadic blacksmiths are often in Birendira plying their trade, with villagers bringing their implements for sharpening or grinding. Against the roar of the temporary furnaces, you hear the ring of metal being struck as the blacksmiths hammer new axe-heads and implements into being.

I always enjoy Birendira, being the crossroads for so much traffic. It was the halt at the end of the sealed road when I first came in 1975 and continued to be so until the mid-eighties, when the road was built to Dhordo and the other villages strung along the route.

Visiting Dhordo in 1984 with my son, Tress, we made an unforgettable journey over Banni to Birendira. Mr Gulbeg kept several jeeps at Dhordo, needing their frequent use as he was in charge of all forty six Banni villages, as I have previously observed. Jeeps were the only practicable vehicles to drive over a roadless terrain. Mr Gulbeg spent many hours on long, dusty journeys visiting his villages and attending Bhuj to confer with local government officials.

Mr Gulbeg was commonly regarded as the king of Banni. He earned this title due to his unremitting service to all the people of Banni. He

Another traditional muslin fabric used in Banni work. Mutwa woman traditionally dressed on right.

was spoken of as being a man with a great heart, and on his death he was greatly mourned, and is still very well remembered.

He told me a lot about the ways of the Banni people, how when his nomadic Arab Bedouin ancestors arrived some four hundred years ago in the wilderness that Banni was then, they roamed freely with their animals, and how the open spaces made them feel the close presence of God. He spoke of how these sturdy men and women were not only sturdy in body but in their spirit, and how the men were tall and well- built, and lived simply and closely with their kin, with their minds free.

There has been a long and affectionate regard by the royal family for the Gulbeg family; in the 1930's Mr Gulbeg's father had an honorary title conferred on him for his services to the Maharao. He bred a very good hunting dog, employed for use in Banni, there being at the time much game there. Mr Gulbeg's title could therefore be consequent upon his father's title before him. As we see in Chapter 8, the present Maharao continued the tradition of having Kutchi hounds from Mr Gulbeg.

In Mr Gulbeg's jeep collection was a very desirable 1940s Wild Willy USA jeep. My son, Tress, spotted it, and asked if we could use it. A Willy jeep is every young man's dream. It is essentially a macho vehicle, chunky and built for desert or rough terrain. This one must have come with the troops in the Second World War. It was a dusty cream version with the star on its bonnet.

The jeep needed some repairs to the engine and was going to be taken to Birendira and to Bhuj to be attended to. We asked if we could come too. It was on tow and we rode in the front with Ali Karim, who was driving. Immediately, we realised our mistake, as the vehicle became engulfed

Shri Gulbeg wearing a Minia Rumal turban. A rumal is a metre square of fabric printed with a resist made of natural ingredients before being dyed with natural dyes, of madder and indigo worn by the Mutwa. This textile is now extinct, as the natural ingredients to make the resist can now not be procured. The resist was made from the seed of the fruit of the Gojoba tree. First the fox ate the fruit and the dung was collected and the seed from the dung then extracted. The seed within the fox underwent a chemical change. A combination of different labour pursuits and the demise of the fox has led to the death of this interesting fabric. The rumal was common is 1975 as was the style of tying the turban.

in the dust thrown up by the jeep towing us. We swaddled ourselves against the dust as much as we could, with only our eyes showing. However, I soon called a halt and changed vehicles, where with the windscreen up and the open sides, the dust pleasantly funnelled past us to land on Tress and Ali Karim.

Arriving at Birendira, we got out and brushed the dust off, but, when Tress and Ali Karim emerged, they were totally unrecognisable. Thickly plastered with dust, they looked just like Egyptian mummies. Coughing the dust out of their lungs, they took off their glasses, exposing ringed eyes and, unwrapping the layers of clothes, filled the air with clouds of dust, seeming to come straight out of a pharaoh's tomb. It is understandable that my son has never forgotten this journey, nor the splendid vehicle.

A memorable story that Mr Gulbeg told me in 1975 was about the smuggling, which went back and forth across the Rann. Gujarat, of which Kutch and Banni are now part, is an alcohol-free state in honour of Mahatma Gandhi, who was born in Gujarat. All the Banni villages fringe the edge of the Rann, which forms the border between Pakistan and India, and in every village in both countries people have relatives. Besides the many ties of kinship, there were other common factors such as pilgrimages to holy pirs, seasonal migration, trade and the strong cultural ties of poetry, which is personified in music and song, which united them, and still does.

Before Partition, people always journeyed to and fro over the Rann on camel-back to visit relatives. Partition did not immediately separate the countries: the border remained porous for several decades. Border controls began to be tightened after the war in 1965, but regular furtive movements of people continued from both sides. With increased tension between the countries, the border began to be sealed and patrolled and was finally sealed in 1980.

However, in 1975 the visiting continued, smuggling back alcohol and other desirable items from Pakistan into Banni. However, the most important

The Kuchie hound, this one is a handsome brindle.

Harijan woman wearing her noserings
put on for a wedding and the
beautiful outstanding embroidery

items smuggled into Pakistan from India were the leaves used for making paan. These were unobtainable in Pakistan and were grown in India. As paan was consumed at this time on a daily basis by most people, there was a hearty trade for this item. In order to outwit any possible capture of the contraband by the camel border patrol, it is said that trained camels crossed the Rann riderless. We will never know the truth of this, but I like the story. But what I did see then and still see today are embroidered articles such as Sindhi caps being sported by some men. There is now an official crossing to visit relatives, and many people make this journey, and presumably bring the Sindhi items back with them.

On the journey back to the village from Bhuj, I noticed many people in twos or threes or more, walking at intervals along the road. Alladin explained that these were pilgrims walking some fifty-plus kilometres to Hajipur, where there was a festival to be held in a few days' time. Hajipur is the site of a holy man (or sufi or pir). People go to get his blessing and are deemed more worthy if they travel on foot. This is very similar to the many pilgrimage sites throughout India for Hindus. Many traditions are similar, or intertwined in their complexity, with the two religions having existed side-by-side for centuries. It is also reminiscent of Christian pilgrimages, the most commonly known to us, of course, being the pilgrimage to Canterbury.

All along the way, places are set up for the pilgrims to rest or sleep. Food stalls are also set up at regular intervals. The pilgrims walk in the cool of the night and in the early morning, as the days are now very hot, with the temperatures in the upper thirties. The Mela (or fair) at Hajipur is famous, with many Muslim pilgrims as well as many Hindus going there to enjoy it.

The road was so different from the road on which I had travelled to Bhuj just a mere two days previously. It had then been empty of people; now we passed hundreds of pilgrims, many people walking and coming from much further afield than Bhuj, which must be some sixty kilometres from Hajipur. In Gujarat, particularly, I have seen Jain pilgrims walking on many pilgrimages, Gujarat being home to many Jains. The most important pilgrimage for Jains is to Palitana, with people walking there from the other end of the state, which may take up to two months.

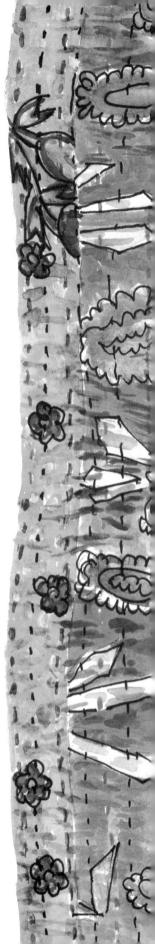

I once met a hearty group of pilgrims who had spent this length of time on their pilgrimage. On the day I was at Palitana, they were celebrating the end of their pilgrimage with a long procession, which included two elephants in fine array and with their holy men carried on silver palanquins. Those on top of the elephants were showering the travellers and the onlookers with money. It was a spectacularly glorious procession.

Jain pilgrims are easy to distinguish as they wear white and cover their noses and mouths with a white cloth, so no insect can meet its death by accident. They wear cloth bindings on their feet, leather not being allowed. The pilgrims we saw on our journey back to the village were walking a full seven days before the Mela started. It makes a break in the daily tedium for many people. Mostly the pilgrims will stay for the three days of the Mela.

The Hajipur Mela goes on for some days and is host to many stalls and rides which are similar to those of a Western fair. One is the Wall of Death, although I think our Western version is rather tamer. Here, cars with the drivers hanging out of the doors are driven up and around the wall, along with another car driven round in the opposite direction. The cars crazily cross each other, while motorbikes weave in and out, all on a vertical wall; added to which, the circular structure is a very rickety affair and seems likely to collapse any minute. I would say that this ride is certainly chancing death.

Curly horned buffalo and cows having a sleep in the noon day sun.

On our return to Dhordo, we found men gathered around the lit-up reception area, smoking and talking. Before Miaw built the tiled seat which runs round the apron in front of the reception building, the men used to sit hunkered down on their haunches, smoking biddies in the dark evening outside the mosque. Now, the social evening gathering has transferred itself to here.

It is always pleasant to stop and see the men having a smoke and a yarn together. I too stopped awhile before saying my good nights, pleased to have been away but glad to be back in what I consider my home in India.

charpoy: a wooden laquered bed circa 1975

Chapter 14

Quilt making

While the art of embroidery diminishes, the art of the quilt still goes forward. It is the one tradition that is common to all the villages, and women in every village in Banni still make quilts.

Quilt-making is a personal expression for every woman in every village, and represents a common artistic and practical pursuit. Because I recognise it as such, I have used quilt motifs, designs and patterns as illustrations throughout the book.

The reason why quilt-making has lasted as this common craft is the practical need for warmth. Quilts are used every day and in greater numbers during the winter period. They form a significant part of any girl's dowry and she will have at least ten newly-made quilts. The number was twenty to twenty-five in 1975 (see dowry list page 226). The girl will have made a significant part of the quilts herself but her mother and other family members will have been busy for years making the quilts against her wedding day. The embroidery may well be executed by a senior family member, as the art of embroidery is declining, while the girl will sew the more pedestrian work.

Quilts are all single-size and have either patchwork or embroidery designs worked into the central panel. The time spent on making a quilt is now generally shorter and a Mutwa quilt will generally not have such rich embroidery as in 1975 and different fabrics now go into its construction, but the overall arrangements of design remains largely the same.

Whereas before many quilts were made from scraps of fabric or old clothes, now most quilts are made from newly-purchased fabrics. As I have said before, the men do all the shopping and will buy all the materials for the women. Accordingly, what the lady has requested and desires in the way of pattern and choice of colour and fabric, may well be changed by what the man chooses and finds in the market place. However, a man does take great care in his purchases, and as he knows the art of the needle and the traditions very well, he chooses with care and thought, and with the requests of his wife, or sister, or mother in mind.

Traditionally, the quilt would be made from natural fabrics with plain colours for the central ground and other patterned or plain colours making up the lines of quilted border. The favoured

Quilt fragment: showing cut patterns common to the villages. The pattern is made by folding together layers of fabric and cutting the pattern out.

traditional fabric for the back of the Mutwa quilt would often be green. Green is the colour of the Muslim flag and stands for Muslim beliefs (whereas orange is the colour for Hindu flag and beliefs). Occasionally, off-white, red or another plain colour may be used as well as patterned fabrics for the back of the quilt, but green is the commonly preferred colour.

In 1975, I found many patterned fabrics in Bhuj, circa 1930. I discovered that the patterns had not been up-dated because of the interruption of the Second World War, which was then followed by Partition. It was cheaper for textile printing firms to just simply continue printing the same designs rather than employ a designer and have the great expense of changing all the screens or rollers. Certainly I felt in 1975 that I had stepped into a time warp. The cotton floral designs were so stylised and from an earlier age as to seem something remarkable. They are still to be found and are still used and have become traditional materials used in their contemporary quilts.

It is heartening to see that this age-old quilt-making craft, though not of the same quality, it still good and being practised in all the Banni villages.

Quilt construction by the Mutwa

The central field of the quilt will be some 100 cm by 140 cm and will be worked first with either embroidery or patterned with patches of applied cut-out designs. If fabric patches are used, these designs are cut out in fabric and then applied by turning under the edges and sewing them down. The patterns always bring to my mind Matisse's cut-paper work which he did in his later years. The ladies in Dhordo cut in expressive ways and with an abstract quality very akin to his work. It is vigorous and spirited and often in bright primary colours. Sometimes a cut fabric border going round the applied field is also made. These borders are made in the fashion of folding and refolding layers of cloth and then cutting the design through.

The most usual tradition is for three or four borders of plain fabric to be applied in a sequence of strips round the field. These will all have small white triangles edging each strip. The triangles point inwards and it has been said that these protect the central image - the person sleeping under the quilt. I asked about this, but was told that the use of triangles was their custom only. It is possible that it originally came from a belief system, but today it is purely tradition. In 1975 the ladies in Dhordo always surmounted each point of the triangle with three small stitches in white thread which also form a triangle. This more lengthy process and finer work has now almost been abandoned.

After these borders, plain or patterned material might run for four more borders. One may be white with diamonds in different colours edging it round. Finally, there is an outer edging border, which is most often in plain white fabric.

Then the quilt is constructed. Using a flat surface, the backing material is first spread out face-side down, then a layer of cotton is spread evenly over this, with the final worked side facing uppermost. The work of stitching the quilt together is made with the face-side of the quilt uppermost. To make the quilt, running stitch in alternating lines of green and red thread, with the lines spaced an inch apart, firmly secure the quilt. This alternate coloured line is the tradition only of the Mutwa community

Other communities have an embroidery pattern or stitch by which they are individually known. The Harijan in particular are known for their

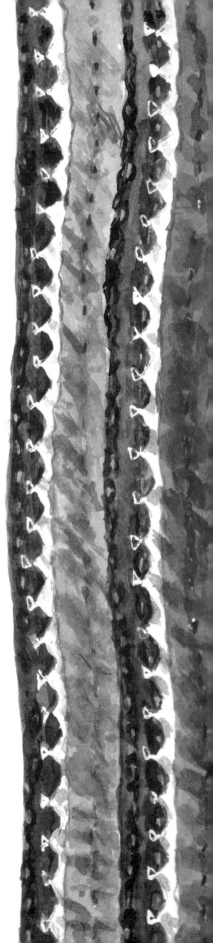

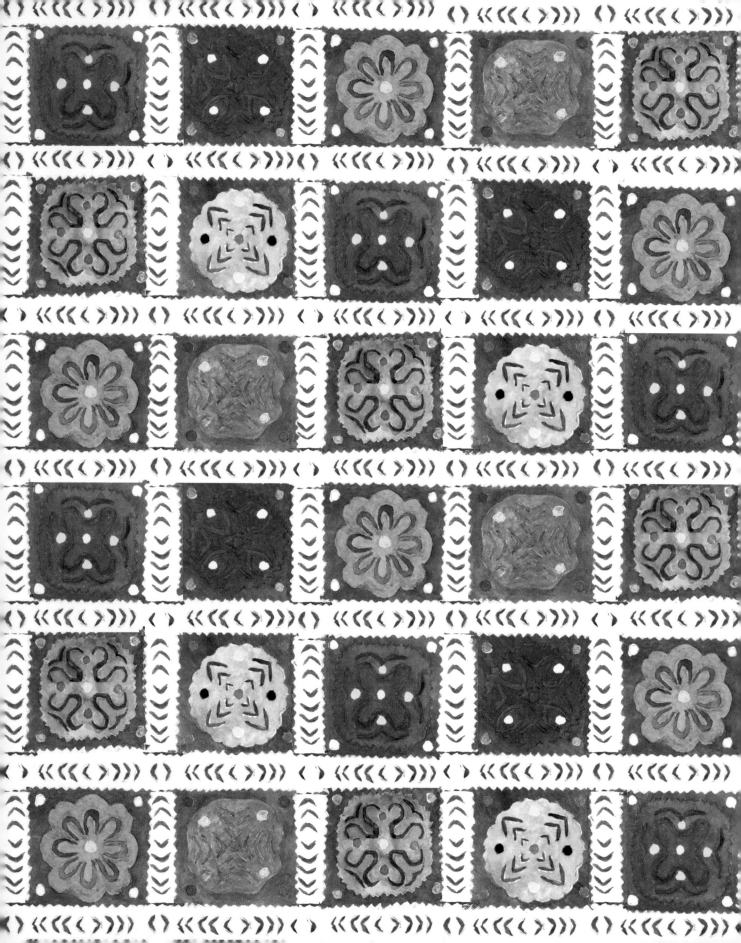

step stitch quilts. The skill of the Harijan embroideries is in executing the step stitch on ordinary mill cloth, not as one would expect on a counted thread fabric. The Harijan community know the stitch so well and they execute it so perfectly that you would think by its appearance it was counted work.

Mutwa embroidery and stitches

The distinctive feature of Mutwa embroidery and of all the Muslim communities throughout Banni is that the patterns they use and have created over the years are all abstract. While in mosques throughout the Muslim world the decoration has been restricted to abstract designs, there are no such restrictions outside the mosque. This is particularly illustrated in the wonderful Persian and Kashmir carpets, which freely use flowers and animals in the fields and borders.

The quilt is a form of carpet in that it uses the field and border concept but differs in the design and images used. I always wonder how, or where, this belief that you use only abstract designs came about, but this belief is very firmly held today as it has always been in this area. This rigid belief applies not only to the quilts, but to every artefact they embroider, be it a blouse top, a pillow piece, a bag or the wedding cover for the face.

Each design they create is given a name, as you can see on page 48.

Stitches used in Mutwa work are few and are commonly known. The stitches used are a lace stitch, which is locally referred to as Gujarati stitch, otherwise known as Maltese Cross, running stitch, chain stitch, ladder chain stitch, back stitch, fine feather stitch, a close herringbone, and buttonhole stitch, making up the entire repertoire. This is not to imply the work is inferior because the stitches used are few and commonplace. It is what they do with the stitches that is magnificent!

I have given working illustrations of the stitches in appendix 3.

Good modern example of an appliquéd cut work quilt

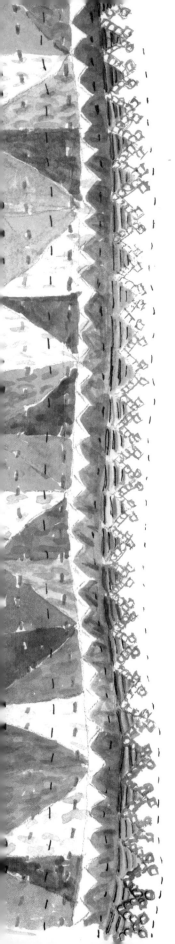

Shisha mirror

The glass blowers in 1975 used to blow their globes of mirror glass for the shisha just outside the walls of the original Bhuj. With the earthquake of 2001 altering and destroying Bhuj so extensively, many people became displaced and sought work elsewhere, and I have not seen this art practised here any more. Shisha mirror glass is now produced and bought from Limdi (Limdi is an hour from Ahmedabad some two hundred miles away). The glass is blown into a globe and, when cool, broken into large pieces. Ladies with scissors and much skill cut and fashion it to different sizes, which are graded by passing the shisha through different sized holed sieves. It can be bought in these various sizes or bought in big pieces. The shisha mirror is sold by weight.

In Dhordo the women cut it for themselves, as they use such small pieces in their embroidery work. They score a line with a pointed stone on the back of the glass to break it into smaller pieces. They then cut it with blunt scissors and smooth the rough sides by rubbing them on a stone or concrete.

Because the glass is broken from a globe, it retains a curved and therefore reflective quality. This can be seen clearly in such communities as the Jat where they use large pieces, often triangular in shape. The curve in the surface, which often has imperfections in it, makes the embroideries glint and flash magnificently in the sun.

Threads and materials

In the quilting tradition, Banni quilts have previously used fabrics predominantly cut from worn garments. It was an artistic use of old garments when new fabrics were beyond a person's means. In 1975 this was much the case in Dhordo, and there were many more beautiful and traditional fabrics in daily use; as these became worn, rather than discard them, the thrifty lady cut the good fabric from them and in the time-honoured way used it again: now this is not the case. Some of the fabrics being reused in 1975 would be Ajrakh, as each man then wore Ajrakh as a lungi, and on his head tied an Ajrakh length into a village turban. Men and women's silk mushru trousers were in most wardrobes and every woman owned tops made from the traditional patterned mushru. Now these traditional fabrics and garments have gone. So, where before these many garments would be cut up and the good fabric used again, this is not happening any more. Other materials from this time would be almost entirely made of cotton.

Nylon and synthetic fabrics have replaced these traditional fabrics, and as they are cheap and soon lose their charm they are discarded and more new cheap fabrics purchased. For the quilts, nylon is often used because of its easy care, along with other synthetic fabrics, but if the piece is to be finely embroidered, then a good plain fabric is bought, which may well be a cotton mixture. Over time, each lady will have collected various fabrics from which she selects her borders.

For the embroidery, synthetic floss silk threads are used. The floss silk was produced in Pakistan and after Partition this trade ceased. It is a simple way of dating a piece of embroidery, the floss being easily recognisable by the way the stitches and embroidery lie flat on the fabric. Floss is several-stranded and not plied, while synthetic silk is twisted and plied and so sits separately on the fabric. Further, if floss has been worked in satin stitch in horizontal and vertical directions, it forms a shading as in velvet.

In the Mutwa community only one fine silken thread is used to execute their fine embroidery, while other communities use two or three threads. The silk comes in skeins and is bought by weight. The husbands or men-folk who are shopping know which merchant has good thread which is dye-fast. If it is not dye-fast, then the art of the needle is lost in washing. Primary colours are mostly favoured, with black and white used for the outlines. Skeins can be divided so the purchaser can buy just a few ounces. Embroidery shops crammed with an array of beads and sequins abound in Bhuj. Various beads are also purchased for certain pieces where a fringe is made, such as in the bag which the bridegroom takes round at a wedding and the wedding veil worn by the man: both are illustrated in chapter nine.

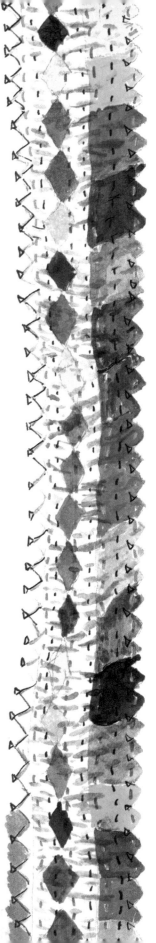

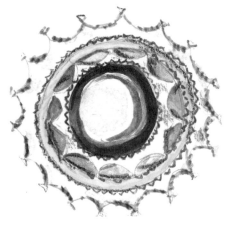

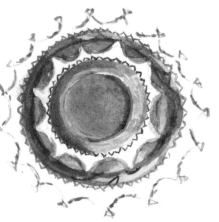

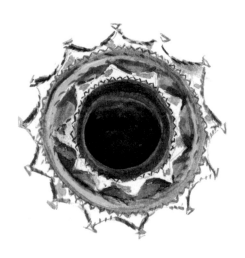

Dowry

Dowry is an age-old custom throughout the world and is the prize or booty accompanying the marriage. Arranged marriages have been practised not only in India but throughout the world. Engagements and affiances were sought at an early age and a young child of three years could be given in a bond of marriage, in India as well as in many countries throughout the world.

Daughters and sons have been used as barter and as pawns in a chess game since time immemorial, and of course arranged marriages amongst Europe's nobility who were seeking alliances with other countries for political gain, family gain and monetary gain were always the custom. As an illustration of this, in 1662 the Portuguese Infanta, Catherine of Braganza, gave Bombay as part of her dowry to Charles the Second of England. A glorious marriage gift, not then fully recognised as such, as at that time Bombay was a group of seven islands.

Here in the village in 1975 I was told that formerly engagements of children were undertaken at the age of three, and sometimes the marriage was conducted between very junior children, but the girl did not go to her husband's family until she menstruated. However, in 1975, while an informal understanding might be made several years before the marriage, the marriage was not conducted before the girl was twenty or so.

Now in the twenty first century, it is common for early negotiations to be made but for the marriages to take place when the couple reach the age of twenty to twenty three. At this age the girl may be given a choice of husband and she is asked to make up her mind, as is the boy.

In 1975 the village dowry was on a more practical and somewhat more modest level than on the high level of the Maharajahs or European courts. I made a list of a bride's expected dowry, and it can be seen, through the list which is representative of the articles in a typical village dowry of 1975, that the girl would have been a gifted embroidress to accomplish all these dowry articles: and this was a most desirable talent. Without this talent and art of her needle, her dowry would have been poor, even though all the family would be embroidering for her marriage for many years. So, from the boy's side, for your betrothed to be a

practised needle-woman was a highly desirable and sought-after talent: and for her it meant she had a greater choice of suitors. You can see by the number of tops and quilts how profuse the use of embroidery was and the importance of this craft in the community. The execution of such a dowry could only be achieved over many years, with the girls and womenfolk in each household working many hours each day, which is indeed what they did, as the average number of hours spent in embroidering each day was six to eight hours on my first visit in 1975.

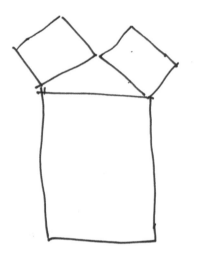

Black and white Mutwa top showing the areas of embroidered designs and how it is made up from four pieces of fabric. Tailoring is not used, it is piece made as follows - two shoulder pieces, angled bodice piece and oblong for lower blouse. Strips are added to the top to bring it round making a sleeve and pieces added to the sides and by tradition tied across the back with strings.

Mutwa dowry lists

1975

21 embroidered choli tops. Some made by herself and others made by her sisters, mother and aunts.

Three embroidered choli tops are given to her by her mother and father in law. These are set pieces: one is made of mushru with shells used in the roundels on the breasts, one is pink and one is on a red ground. The cut of these pieces is different with no triangular insertion at the bust level (see illustration).

Ordanies are given by the girl's parents. One is in tie and dye, one is black or white and the others are patterned.

Two pairs of mushru trousers. These were vast and wide like a bridge.

One pair of marriage earrings in gold or silver as they can afford.

One pair of silver anklets.

Bride gives her husband one ring for his fourth finger. Girl's parents give her eight brass water pots.

Parents give her large married women's nose ring.

Mother-in- law gives one embroidered top made in mushru material.

Bride's mother gives her 20-23 quilts Bride will have been making these with her Mother.

Groom's parents give her 5 or so quilts

Groom's parents give her a new house.

Groom's parents give the new daughter in law one pair of shoes made by the Hairjans

Groom's family give her five or so cows or buffalo

2009

10 quilts

Set of gold earrings

Silver anklets

Three ordanies

Groom's parents give her a new house

Wrist watch

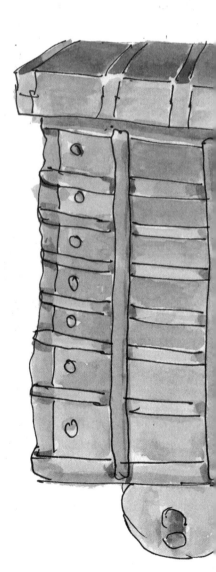

It is apparent there is a sharp difference in the dowry of 1975 and in the embroidery produced then and now. The choli top is the most significant garment to have gone. In the 1975 list we see some 24 pieces; these interestingly enough were full-backed cholies, though backless ones were worn, and I saw ladies wearing them. However, you were only permitted to wear them over the age or 45 and thought to be unattractive - while when you were young and desirable you had to be modest in your attire. There is also a total demise of the gift of cows or buffaloes, which bears witness to the lack of grassland and the changing job pursuits.

In 1975, dowry chests were commonly bought by the girls family and gradually filled with her dowry. Now, this is not needed for the light transport of her dowry items. The rich treasure trove of time past has now irrevocably gone.

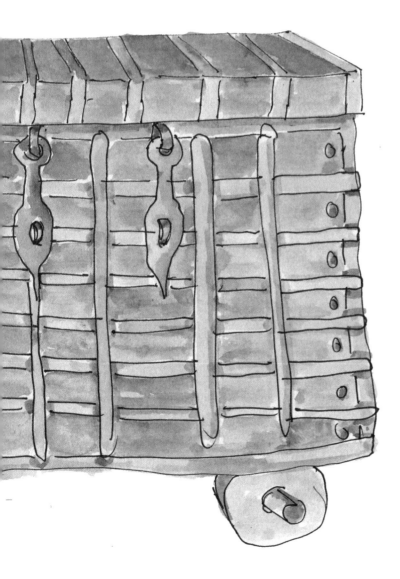

Two lines of embroidery. The stitch is close herringbone and is used to join two fabrics together.

Banded metal dowry chest typical of Kutch and sometimes used in Banni.

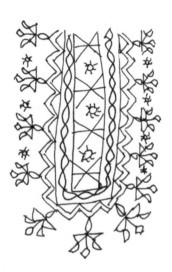

So, what has replaced the time spent in embroidery? Interestingly enough, we find the ladies sitting and embroidering as before, though in fewer numbers and for less hours, but what are they embroidering? On closer inspection we see it is a sari length, an item which Dhordo ladies will never wear. Commercial outlets have sprung up: in fact the seeds of the commercial cottage industry were being sown when I was here in 1975. I foresaw then that commercial interest would ring the death knell on the traditional Mutwa embroidery evolved over centuries. The tradition of the practice of sewing has Persian and Balushistan origins (where several of the Banni communities migrated from) and must have evolved in Banni over at least 400 years to have attained such a peak of excellence.

That the embroidery has evolved is apparent from the old pieces Poppeli and Hulbai brought out for me to see. The pieces were made in about 1900, as they were executed by their grandparents and their generation. These show a former even more minute and exquisite style than is embroidered now and in 1975. To execute them the person must have been young with perfect eyesight. All the early pieces also show a softness of colour as the threads are all vegetable dyed, with the designs using more thread work on the ground.

While I regret the passing of the individual artistic expression, and miss seeing the glorious raiments every man, woman and child previously wore, I recognise that India is changing with great speed into a modern society - where such attire might be thought old-

Black and white designs used in Mutwa embroidery can be seen to be closely copied and used by the Khatri ajrakh block printers as shown in the design on the right. Textile on right made for Indian market.

Kutoree Pukee chopal

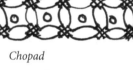

Chicken   *Chicken*

Chopad   *Chopad*

Boutee Gukako   *Boutee Ticken*

Chicken

Chicken

Chicken

Chicken

Chicken and pako

fashioned. Perhaps the younger lady without realising it feels the mood of change, and no longer wants to be different in her village dress!

Whatever it is, commercial interests can only have hastened what might very possibly have been destined to happen. The art of embroidery in the village is an oral tradition, colours and patterns being passed down through the generations. Differences of dress, patterns, stitches, colours used in set combinations, set them apart and distinguished them from the other communities in Banni. In every aspect of attire they strove to be different. Earrings, necklaces, nose rings, bangles and the distinctive cut of their garments, each and every item distinguished their community. This distinction was striven for and people took great pride in it. As each school child proudly wears the uniform of their respected school, so the villagers wore their own distinctive garments.

Commercial interest can and has hastened change from this tradition. Very soon all the traditional garments will become history and not even the colours or patterns will be remembered by the villagers. The vibrant

Nanima sewing a quilt

Quilted bag, made from an old ajrakh textile.

colours which stand out as a blaze in the dun-coloured Banni landscape will be forgotten as the village lady is given silks and fabric of another colour range, designed for the town and city dweller. Unfortunately, the Mutwa have been singled out for commercial interest as they embroider to the town lady's desire, in that the work is truly miniature and perfectly executed. Each stitch is a pleasure to the eye, with the minute shisha safe from breakage because of its very tiny size, and held in place with minute buttonhole stitches.

It must be true that the small amount of rupees paid for the work give a lady some independent money for herself. The government also give master craftsmen awards and more than one lady from Dhordo has been awarded this treasured prize. The excellence of the Mutwa stitch-work is highly thought of and indeed speaks for itself.

What is the future for Mutwa embroidery? I think that it will only survive if the villagers can be seen to work once again with the historic fabrics such as mushru (or good quality cottons) and be able to record their distinctive patterns and colours. I believe there is a commercial market for their very own work and I have proved this with the project I ran with the two villages. I have also shown success with Nanima's embroidered quilt piece embroidered on the historic mushru fabric I gave her, and which she promptly sold to one of my tourists.

Let us be hopeful.

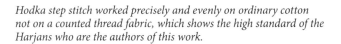

Hodka step stitch worked precisely and evenly on ordinary cotton not on a counted thread fabric, which shows the high standard of the Harjans who are the authors of this work.

Shyly smiling Harijan girl in 1975

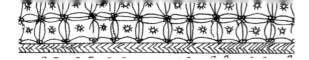

Chapter 15

Future of the village

Subtly, the changes to the village have seeped in through the years and into the pages of this book since my first visit in 1975. The modern world is reaching out and pulling Dhordo into its orbit. In 1975, the isolation of the village protected its traditions from the rest of changing India, but the impregnation of change travelled to the villagers down the new road made in 1984. A road built for their protection against Pakistan brought invasion from another direction.

Horses and, much more significantly, camels were exchanged for jeeps and cars. The camels decked with bright coverings, with household goods on their backs, and others being ridden at a fast pace over Banni, is a vision fused with this landscape which has gone forever, as has the grass. The jeep and the odd vehicle were already there in 1975, but it was a long, dusty trail over Banni to the village and only the very occasional visitors came. Now, in greater and greater numbers, people travel the road and come in faster and faster vehicles over a road which was originally of narrow one-vehicle width. Now the road is constantly being widened as men daily leave the village in pursuit of jobs outside the village and its herding tradition, and much traffic of buses, lorries, cars, jeeps and people ride the roads. Tourists are invited to stay in a new government hotel in Hodka village, some six miles away from Dhordo.

I always found going to Dhordo exciting, and for me travelling in an open jeep with the breeze in my hair crossing the expanse of dusty Banni was the height of pleasure. And I remember in 1975, as you rode along in the warm keen air, you had the sensation that the world was standing still and life would last for ever.

Now, there is commerce and milk production, where formally only breeding and herding was practised. However, the buffalo is not taken into Banni as before (where a herdsman could be gone with the herd for several days following the grass), as the grass is now not sufficient, and modern feeding stuffs are brought into the village. In the West we are guilty of penning cows in stalls and just feeding them for milk production, whereas at least these animals are fed in the village and are then free to roam.

As the world shrinks and far off-places become sought after in the age-old quest for adventure and exploration, so travellers are lured to these once remote and now semi-remote villages. It is an interesting exchange. As the villagers reach out for the modern world with restaurants and different foods to refresh the palette, and cladding the body with modern shirts and dresses, they are unwittingly casting off their centuries-old culture.

But other customs such as marriage and significant ceremonies such as the circumcision of a boy at the age of seven are still firmly adhered to.

I recently witnessed the ceremonies following a boy's circumcision celebrated by the men and women in separate ceremonies. The celebration took place about a week after the circumcision. A group of men went to the house of the boy, where he was dressed in a new costume with a sword by his side and a turban on his head, with a veil of beads tied round this and hanging over his face. The men conducted him to the village hall, where all the village men were sitting on mats spread on the floor. The boy sat on the floor facing the headman. Religious prayers were recited and the headman went through the ceremony with the boy giving his responses. A second gold turban was then set over the first, and then, to bring it up to date, and - which certainly added joy to the ceremony - a necklace of flashing lights was placed round his neck. This is an important marker in a boy's life: it is part of his journey to manhood. The boy then rose and everybody gave him money. In my picture you see the boy with his beaded veil thrown back and the money pinned to his shirt. Here he collected money in a vessel. The men conducted him back to the women, who had gathered in all their finest clothes and had been enjoying themselves singing and talking. They then each gave the boy money, followed by a feast served to everybody. The men were in their part and the women in theirs, with the boy allowed to wander where he wished.

What of the village family members I have known since 1975, Mrs Gulbeg, the surviving widow of Mr Gulbeg, Poppeli, Miaw, and Ali Akbar, their three children? Mrs Gulbeg will spend her remaining days sitting in her family compound sewing quilts for her family. I bring her long-eyed needles as she can no longer see to thread the small-

Preceding page Harijan girl in 1975 with the hairstyle worn by all girls and ladies in 1975. She has her community's earrings, two necklaces both traditional, the lower is a necklace of amulets containing good wishes for her, and her bracelets and anklet together with her richly embroidered top.

Boy at his celebration programme following his circumcision at the age of seven. Money has been pinned to the front of his garment.

FUTURE OF THE VILLAGE

eyed needles. She sits quietly sewing as her grandchildren and now her great grandchildren greet her each day. A truly respected matriarch. Poppeli, her handsome eldest daughter, a strong woman to have taken the burden at her father's death in becoming the head-woman, served the village well for three years. She has had a long and happy marriage to Abdul Karim, her first cousin, and has had nine children out of her desired packet of children (a packet is eleven).

Night of the New Moon, a book written about Muslim Women in India by Anees Jung, published in 1993, includes a story about Poppeli, and the following quote sums up some of the beliefs at this time, which in fact are still held, though subtly changing now that there is greater exposure to city culture. Here is her voice. "In Banni we are isolated from those corrupting influences and we are together. Our community will not accept a girl from outside. If an outsider comes, the bond is weakened. If they come from good stock the marriage is good. If the wall is strong then the picture which

Old man wearing his Ajrakh turban.

hangs on it will be good. We live within the perimeters of the clan. As we never leave the village we have not begun to think differently. What the clan thinks sub-consciously becomes out thoughts."

Of marriage, Poppelie tells us, "However good a woman is, it is a man who is King; he is her Taj." Abdul Karim has been her King.

Abdul Karim sought work outside the village and worked at the factory for years and became a manager. For a hobby he breeds the Mewar horse and is a judge, going to shows throughout Gujarat and into Rajasthan. Now he and Poppelie have stepped right outside their traditional family pursuits and in 2011 purchased a farm outside Banni which has its own assured water from a bore well. Never before has a Banni villager become a landowner.

Poppelie still embroiders, not very much on her own work, but is daily to be seen working on pieces of commercial work. She is well aware of all the big changes and the different lives now being led, which she fears will break the common bond of the harmonious village life with its simple daily round.

Ali Akbar, Mr Gulbeg's second son, is still a very necessary auxiliary doctor to the surrounding hamlets and villages, especially those not favoured by the connecting roads. His musician son, Alladin, follows a different career and works as a guide to the villages for the travellers coming into Banni. His sister, Sifyer, is a gifted embroidress and now trains several ladies to produce articles for travellers coming to the village. While I was in Dhordo last winter two women came into the village to promote women's health and wanted a lady to volunteer for training in Bhuj. To my astonishment, Sifyer has accepted this role and for the very first time she will be going outside her village (stepping outside her own self-imposed purdah) on her own. This is a momentous decision.

Miaw Hussein, now the Headman, the youngest son of Mr Gulbeg, has also significantly moved from the Banni herding tradition, and has become a very successful business man. He owns a bore well outside Banni. He has two lorries and supplies the factory on the Rann with water on a daily basis. With his own money he has financed many projects, most notably the free eye hospital which comes to all the Banni villages bi-annually, and is dedicated to his father's memory.

I have spoken only of the central family, showing the radical change in their lives from the centuries-old traditional pursuit of

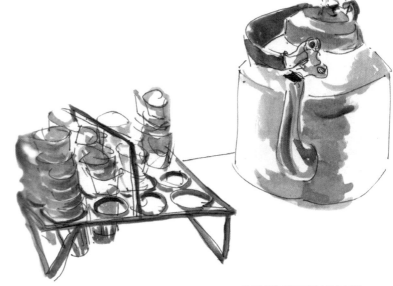

Chai kettle and glasses.

Young boy with his sunburnt hair. To protect the hair from the sun, it is oiled and covered, as bleached hair is not favoured. He is wearing the patterned scarf now favoured by the present generation in Banni.

Right: embroidered patterned border in silver.

breeding cattle, but this change is reflected in every village household, and the pastoral way of life which I witnessed in 1975 has gone forever.

What of education for the village children? In 1975 there was no school in Dhordo, although there was a junior school in Gorivali (three miles away). Because the villages were so isolated the quality of the teachers was poor. The good teachers did not want to go to live in villages without any plumbing or modern conveniences, and with no social life. On a number of occasions I would go to the village schools scattered in Banni and find no teacher there, as he or she had absconded and was often absent or semi-permanently absent, having gone back home. The teacher's stipend was also very low, although a town teacher would improve his income by giving private lessons, whereas this was not possible in the villages. In all the village schools there was also a nearly total absence of equipment, with only slates and chalk commonly found. Every year that I visited Banni I took school items, often wind-up radios and educational toys for the village schools.

Life has a complex pattern and the connection with my travelling to India becomes fascinatingly and unexpectedly interwoven with my ancestry. I have often wondered if we are born with a blue-print of our past ancestors' lives, like a talent where all the children become actors or explorers, or such as inheriting a family resemblance like the shape of a nose or the colour of the hair. In the same way, maybe some members of the next generation will live the lives of their ancestors and be led mysteriously and inexorably to once again live or work in the same continent.

I speak, of course, of myself, where I have so frequently, especially in India, had the sensation of déjà vu. I was a child of a broken marriage, my parents having separated when I was a baby at the outbreak of the Second World War, which also contributed to the separation of the two families. I was brought up knowing nothing of my father's family.

I came to India in 1975 and only subsequently found to my fascination that my paternal great grandfather was born at Cawnpore (now spelt Kanpur) and all his eight siblings were born either at Agra, Cawnpore, Jhansi, Ambala or Shimla and that my great grandfather was General

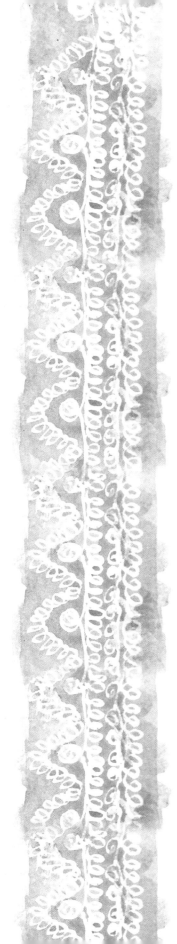

FUTURE OF THE VILLAGE

Mutwa girl at the well — behind
her is a piece of silver work in a traditia

John Nicholas Tresidder, I.M.S (Indian Medical Service). My great grandfather was not a military man but a doctor. He went out to India as a Captain, and his rise through the ranks was helped and promoted by the important role he played at Cawnpore, from where the Indian Mutiny started. My great grandfather, Dr John Nicholas Tresidder, was the physician to the Rajah of Cawnpore, whose dispute with the British over the pension of £80,000 paid to his father being stopped on his father's death (he was an adopted son and therefore was not regarded by the British as a direct heir) was central to the mutiny. On the anniversary of the battle at Plassey, 23rd June 1857, the Rajah led his men to a major assault on the residency at Cawnpore, with resulting horrific atrocities. Dr John Nicholas Tresidder was called to Gwalior by Lord Canning in an attempt to identify the missing Rajah. The Rajah was never found. My great grandfather being asked to describe his character said of him, "He was an extremely uninteresting fellow." My great grandmother was also the first woman to return to Cawnpore after the atrocities. My ancestors lived in India at a very momentous time in its history. Dr John Nicholas Tresidder was also an early photographer, and he recorded not only his own family but also the life and times he lived in. Being stationed in Cawnpore at the time of the mutiny, his photographs bear witness to this, and help form an important record of this time. A portfolio of his photographs is in the Alkazi Arts Foundation in Delhi.

I therefore feel that when I visit the Taj Mahal I am definitely treading on my ancestors' footprints, as being stationed in Agra they must have visited the Taj many times and most possibly have danced there, as the Taj was not respected as the monument it now is, and dances were conducted on the terrace. I often wonder at the lives they must all have lived. My great grandfather went out to India in 1845, while it was still the East Indian Trading Company, before coming under the Crown and the British Raj in 1858, the year following the mutiny. On his retirement to England he called his house Cawnpore. My grandfather born in India was duly educated in England, but recognized that India influenced him throughout his life.

Certain it is that India holds my attention and fills my soul with joy, as I am sure it did for my ancestors. What of my children brought here so adventurously in 1975? I wonder at myself, seeing with hindsight the potential folly of such an action. They have all travelled back to India and they are still writing their histories, and it will be for them to tell.

Meanwhile, before we say good-bye to the village, what of the daily round of the ladies? Poppeli's voice is here as she says, "Lorna, now the ladies have everything, they have running water in their homes and modern furniture, concrete on the floor outside their houses, and electricity

This man has such a wonderful smile, striding after his buffalo in the Banni landscape.

244

with fans, lights and fridges, and television in many homes. In 1975 we had nothing; now every family has work with money coming in." But she is also concerned about the changes and the disruption to the tight bonds of a common life shared by all. These ties of kinship are still there but she is worried that, with the many new diverse jobs and the allure of the city, people will leave the village.

I was accosted in Bhuj by a bright youth. "Hello Lorna. You do not remember me?" Yes I did. Some five years back he was in school in the village and had recited a long poem for my group. I asked him what he was doing and he said he had left his village some three months back and was working as a waiter. His next words sum up his changed life but his sentiments about his village. "I am already missing my village and want to go back to my friends and family."

The embroidery is disappearing, and I miss it. I miss the grass roofs which have been replaced by tiles, and concrete replacing the mud platforms the houses stand on. I miss the spread fingers in the many hand-prints patting the mud of the platform refreshed each week. Above all, I miss all the rich intact culture I witnessed in 1975, the embroidery on every back and the Ajrakh dhotie around the men's bodies and wound round their heads.

But these are a thriving people and with the grass gone they must use common sense and move with the times and change their jobs, and this they are doing. It would not be sensible for young people not to want the electricity and not

to be part of modern India. The embroidery is still there but you must look harder for it. I have been favoured to know these people, and to continue knowing them, and seeing how their lives progress is a privilege..

There are common centuries-old bonds forged with the neighbours in former isolation. I think these bonds, like the imprinted stamp the lives of my ancestors have made on my life, will make an imprint for continued kinship and concord amongst all the village members and their neighbours.

Though these recollections have taken so long to narrate, they took but a little while to pass through my head, as finally we say goodbye to Alladin and wish his embroidered carpet of life to fly well, and the rich tapestry of Dhordo village to continue with its many lives enfolded in firm kinship.

But my last words I set aside to hear once again the words of Shri Gulbeg, my host in 1975 and my friend for many years. "When people live on a wide empty earth with no closed spaces, with the heaven and stars above and the earth below, they live very near to God. Nothing rests in our hands; God holds the strings of our lives. We come empty-handed and we go empty-handed. To serve our fellow man is the only purpose in life - Inshallah."

*Jat girl in 1975 with her under-turned Banni hairstyle
and her shy smile behind her nose ring brings back
yesterday as though it was today.*

Appendices

Harijem embroidery

Community migrations into Banni

Some four to five hundred years ago, the Mutwa ancestors of the villagers of Dhordo migrated from Persia (now Iran), coming into Banni through Sindh. It is said that they followed a holy man. A benign maharajah gave them permission to settle in the grasslands, as they were breeders of cattle. Other Muslim migratory pastoralist groups coming into India over the centuries were also given permission to settle in Banni, as were Hindu people of mainly Harijan caste. Over the centuries, different Muslim holy men went amongst the Hindu village groups and some converted to the Muslim faith. These people are called Arraf. There is now a great predominance of the Muslim faith over the Hindu faith in Banni, with ninety per cent being Muslim.

The Hindu and Muslim groups illustrate the congruence possible between groups with disparate historical and religious backgrounds. Muslims have always regarded Harijans as equals, not as untouchables. Traditions and customs have been cross-fertilised between the two distinct belief systems. The most notable is the Hindu caste system, where marriage is not allowed between the different castes. Muslims in Banni have embraced this rigid rule, and no Muslim marries outside his or her community. The other custom practised by both faiths is the tradition of dowry. This custom, practised by the Hindu, has also been adopted by the Muslims in the Banni villages.

Each community, whether Muslim or Hindu, takes great pride in their oral history of settlement and migration into Banni. Common to all the settlers, except the Harijans, has been their means of livelihood being derived from herding domestic animals, with each community selecting one particular breed of animal as its speciality. Accordingly, some communities were known for camel breeding, others for sheep, goat, cow, or buffalo or combinations of these, and all were dependent on the grasslands.

All the migratory groups coming into Banni travelled to and settled first in Sindh. Dhordo village still has relatives in Sindh, as have many other Banni communities. As said before, when I came in 1975 it was reputed that much illegal trade and commerce of prohibited goods came over the Rann, which divides the same related communities and the two countries.

The Banni communities, who traditionally earned their living from herding animals, are called Maldheri. The Mutwa community, which is the community of Dhordo village, is the most important group, being the oldest and strongest community. Alladin's family have the surname Morani and are the most distinguished premier family of the Mutwa community. Due to the close ties with the royal family, Alladin's great grandfather at the time of Partition, with the division of the countries and therefore of the Mutwa community, chose to stay in Banni, and in India.

The main communities in Banni

Adivasi

the ancient people who are believed, in a similar way to the aborigines, to be the original inhabitants. These people are found in pockets all over India. They were animists and this group converted to the Muslim faith only in the last century. They are known as the Pathans. They are mostly carpenters.

Bamba Muslim

these are only one big village, Misriyada, they breed horses, raise a variety of cattle. Not specialist in any one pursuit.

Haliputra Muslim

settling some 300 years ago, these people came from Sindh and were originally Hindu but then converted to the Muslim faith. They herd buffalo and cow.

Harijan Hindu

The Harijans traditionally earned their living by dealing with the dead animals, tanning the leather hides for the herding communities. They made leather goods from the hides, and settled at different times in many villages throughout Banni. In Hodka village they represent a large, robust community. In 1975, they made wonderful special ceremonial shoes for all the communities, with intricate interwoven silver and plastic threaded lines. Nowadays, not much leather work is produced; they trade more in embroideries made for the commercial market. The Harijan will work for different Muslim households in the same village, doing household jobs like sweeping, cleaning, fetching water and shopping. The women also earn rupees by executing excellent mud-work decoration.

Jat Muslim

settling some 250 years ago, they are reputed to have migrated from Persia, now Iran, through Afganistan, through the North West Frontier into Pakistan and then through Sindh and into Kutch, and first brought camels into this area. This was a hearty trade and the breed of camels coming from this area was famous, being used for riding and the transport of goods. Banni could then support the breeding herds of many camels.

Jat

The Jat are, I would say, the next most distinguished group to the Mutwa. They, like the Mutwa, bear different surnames and distinguish themselves by different embroidery styles. The Jat divided into three groups and have settled and follow different trades. Fakirana Jat have settled in eastern Kutch at Lakpat and Malia following fishing and the raising of camels. Gracia Jat are farmers, while Dhaneta Jat settled in Banni and raised buffaloes and some camels. The women in all three groups wear the black dress but with different embroidery to distinguish one from the other. I have only illustrated the Banni Dhaneta Jat.

Kalar Muslim

a small community found as a enclave in various villages, they breed buffalo and goats.

Kora Muslem

only some 500-600 people settled in villages in the East of Banni on the cusp of the big Rann and the small Rann. If the monsoon favours the little Rann, they take their herds there, and vice versa. The Kora migrated down along the line of the Thar Desert from Rajasthan. The Thar Desert divides Pakistan from India along the borders of Rajasthan.

Mutwa Muslim

breeders of cows, migrating some 400 to 500 years ago from Saudi Arabia to Persia (now Iran) through Pakistan and through Sindh and into Kutch. They came as warriors and mercenaries and as such were given permission to stay on the borders of Kutch and Sindh on the understanding they would protect the border. So they became a security for the King's border. They settled and took up the raising of cows. Many early weapons and firearms were in the possession of Shri Gulbeg, which he donated to the Kutch museum, where they can be found.

Node Muslim

they live only in three villages in Banni but are to be found in other communities in Kutch.

Pathan Muslim

converted from Hindu, coming from Rajasthan, rearing young cows and buffalo for other communities. They are known for their gold and silver embroidery.

Raisiputra Muslim

settling some 300 years ago, mainly settled at Birendira as herders and breeders of sheep.

Sumra Muslim

formerly Hindu and converted to Islam. They originally came from Rajasthan.

Historical episodes

Kutch is a fabled, isolated land, subdivided and ruled by many warring princes of both Muslim and Hindu belief for many centuries. Sindh was Kutch's nearest and natural enemy, and a state of war perpetually existed between the adjoining factions which composed this land mass and their princes, finally becoming two adjoining kingdoms in the seventeenth century. Since the seventeenth century, when Kutch was united into one kingdom, the same dynasty has ruled until the present day, or until Partition, and is still the title holder.

Some features which mark Kutch out as a special kingdom within India are markedly interesting and different. In my selection I have given emphasis to the textiles and to other aspects of religion and customs which have all helped shape the village traditions, their embroidery and their culture, and which give added richness to the preceding chapters.

Kutch has a long and important maritime history of swift, small ships, manned by small crews of sturdy, skilled sailors: seamanship is a salient feature of this land. Small craft set off from these shores in the time of the Pharaohs, with cargoes for the coast of Africa, from Oman down to Zanzibar, and up to the Middle East. Textiles were a great source of export, India having the art of mordanting centuries before Europe (mordanting is dye fixing or making dye fast) and produced bright vegetable-based colours.

Patterning the fabric was also a sophisticated Kutchi art, with the wooden block in repeat patterns being executed in designs which are still in the vocabulary of the block printer today. Ajrakh, vegetable resist dyed fabrics from Kutch dating back to the 5th Century AD, have been found in tombs near Cairo in Egypt; a collection of these early textiles is in the Ashmolean Museum in Oxford. The designs can be seen as the ancestors of the present-day Ajrakh prints being produced in Kutch, and are almost the same patterns as those worn in the village today.

The next high export of textiles comes centuries later in the seventeenth century. Designs which were known as "the tree of life" were hand-painted and then block-printed in Ajrakh block prints (resist block prints) onto cotton and finished with a glaze, and were then exported in greater and greater quantities as these designs became the vogue in England and Europe. Samuel Pepys wrote on 5 September 1663, "Creed, my wife and I to Cornhill, and after many tryalls bought my wife a chintz (a painted calico) for to line her new study, which is very pretty".

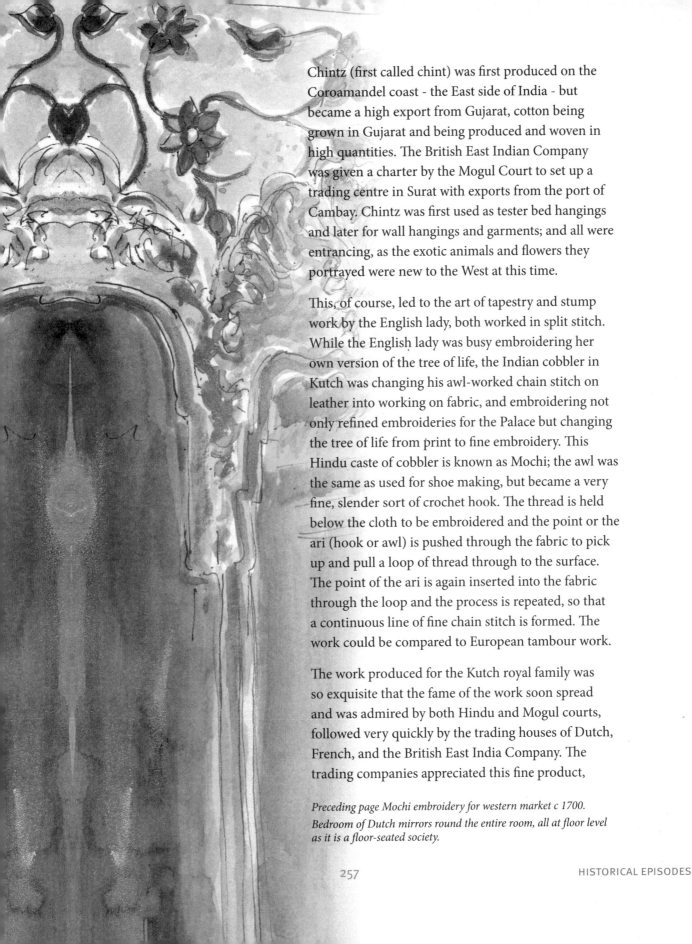

Chintz (first called chint) was first produced on the Coroamandel coast - the East side of India - but became a high export from Gujarat, cotton being grown in Gujarat and being produced and woven in high quantities. The British East Indian Company was given a charter by the Mogul Court to set up a trading centre in Surat with exports from the port of Cambay. Chintz was first used as tester bed hangings and later for wall hangings and garments; and all were entrancing, as the exotic animals and flowers they portrayed were new to the West at this time.

This, of course, led to the art of tapestry and stump work by the English lady, both worked in split stitch. While the English lady was busy embroidering her own version of the tree of life, the Indian cobbler in Kutch was changing his awl-worked chain stitch on leather into working on fabric, and embroidering not only refined embroideries for the Palace but changing the tree of life from print to fine embroidery. This Hindu caste of cobbler is known as Mochi; the awl was the same as used for shoe making, but became a very fine, slender sort of crochet hook. The thread is held below the cloth to be embroidered and the point or the ari (hook or awl) is pushed through the fabric to pick up and pull a loop of thread through to the surface. The point of the ari is again inserted into the fabric through the loop and the process is repeated, so that a continuous line of fine chain stitch is formed. The work could be compared to European tambour work.

The work produced for the Kutch royal family was so exquisite that the fame of the work soon spread and was admired by both Hindu and Mogul courts, followed very quickly by the trading houses of Dutch, French, and the British East India Company. The trading companies appreciated this fine product,

Preceding page Mochi embroidery for western market c 1700.
Bedroom of Dutch mirrors round the entire room, all at floor level as it is a floor-seated society.

HISTORICAL EPISODES

and bed covers, scarves, chintz trees of life and fine cotton European garments were made for the foreign market. The delicate cotton fabric was very desirable and unknown in the West. It may be the embroideries were not exported from the four main ports in Kutch and, if not, they were carried through Gujarat to the port of Cambay to be shipped. Such was the desirability of the Mochi embroidery that many other Mochi embroidery centres outside Kutch came into being. These had patterns which were produced over and over again in many different colourways.

Within the Kutch court, wall panels which lined the walls up to waist-high were embroidered, as well as women's choli (blouse) tops, which were worn with circular skirts wider at the hem than a full circle. The designs were delicate buttis (in the West we would know this as a paisley motif), floral motifs and delicate traceries of flowers derived from Persian carpet and Mogul origins.

Two carpets of Mochi work are known to be in existence today - but more may well have been made. The dimensions make them something to be marvelled at: they are approximately 6 metres wide and 20 metres long. It is an extraordinary feat of needlework; one was made for the Aina Mahal palace in Bhuj and the other one was exported to Hardwick Hall in Yorkshire. The carpet in the Palace in Kutch has only been used twice at Divali (the festival of light). It has a little wax where a candle has spilled. It is a thin carpet and has to be by the delicacy of the work. The palace carpet would have been trodden on by bare feet, as is the Indian custom, but one wonders who were the people at Hardwick Hall who did the treading and how their feet were shod. Both carpets are in very good order and are held in great esteem.

I have talked about this needlecraft to emphasise the importance of embroidery as an embellishment at all levels of society throughout the kingdom. The art of the needle can be seen to have evolved from a folk art to a courtly art in Kutch.

Travellers who passed through Sindh and Kutch came in great numbers over the centuries, bestowing different religious beliefs, habits and traditions, which have given Kutch its distinct flavour. Many tribes or groups coming from Sindh were not benign but were warring

Two views of the Aina Mahal above shows a fret worked window for the ladies of Zanana to look out of.

factions and over the centuries some would emerge and become strong princes, ruling areas within Kutch and, as already said in Appendix 1 (Migration), these warring factions gradually became one kingdom in Kutch and another kingdom in Sindh.

In Kutch, a caste called Jadeja Rajputs became the strongest and forged the kingdom of Kutch. The foundation stone of this dynasty was laid formally in 1604 in Bhuj, and it is still honoured.

Kutchi Architecture was also distinct and, although destruction through successive earthquakes has been devastating, the beautiful Aina Mahal (built in 1760) in Bhuj, with the yet older Palace next to it, has survived, though badly damaged. The older palace next to the Aina Mahal, the Durbar Gadh, is in my estimation a purer architectural style, as it derives no influence from the West and very little from other forms of architecture existing in India at the time it was built. It has very beautiful, huge, wooden fret-worked windows that you find nowhere else in India. They front the rooms of the zeenana, the women's harem, the windows allowing the ladies to see out but not be seen.

The foundation stone of the dynasty is in a building adjacent to this palace, which dates the palace to the early 17th century.

The Aina Mahal was brought into being through a talented gentleman called Ram Singh Malam. As a young man, he was sailing out from Kutch to the coast of Africa as a merchant seaman. His ship was destroyed in a storm, and he was rescued by a ship sailing to Holland, where he stayed for several years, becoming a skilled craftsman in glass and many other subjects, before taking passage back to Kutch.

The King, Maharao Lakpati, an enlightened, educated man, saw the advantages this gifted man could bring to his court, and sent him back to Holland with a group of craftsmen to learn the crafts of the West - architecture, glass, enamel work and Dutch blue tiles being some of the learned crafts.

Through this valuable link with the West, many items were imported and the influence of the returned craftsmen can be seen in the contents of the museum and in the building. Coloured glass was made and used; Belgian glass mirrors abound in strange arrangements; and clocks from

the West were a passion. With a twist of humour, sculptures of Dutch men dressed in their European coats and tricolour hats complete with angels' wings grace the gateway and entrance to the Aina Mahal.

Because the Kingdom of Kutch was geographically separated by the narrow neck of land from India, and by the Rann from Sindh, it developed over the centuries its very own individuality. A list of the distinct differences of the Kingdom has already been given by His Highness in Chapter 8. But it is the British who recognized and regarded and reported Kutch as having the distinctive features of a separate Kingdom, due in particular to its having its own language, Kutchi, and its own mint and coinage, law, time, and customs.

In 1816, Kutch became an independent princely state during the rule of the British and became part of India, when it gained independence in 1947. With the creation of India and Partition, the currency changed to the rupee, and so the dingla and korree, two coins used for centuries in Kutch, disappeared forever. Folk songs are still sung today telling of the lost dingla "and where has my korree gone"!

In return for British sovereignty, the British gave autonomy; the local factions were harmonised, and a small garrison was maintained with the Residency at Anjar. In 1816 Captain McMurdo was initially sent on a political mission to Kutch to dissuade the ruler from giving shelter to the pirates who infested the North Western Frontier of the Bombay territories. In 1817 he was promoted to the post of political residency in Kutch. However, it was many years before the piracy was controlled. The hardy Kutchi seamen turned pirates for quicker gain, and continued to plague the coast and the British for many years, the Rao resisting imposing the high penalties which were needed to bring it under control.

Coming back again to the period when the East India Company first came to Kutch, we have Mrs Postans informing us that "*after*

Two Dutch cherubs in frock coats and wings which grace the entrance to the Aina Mahal

many years of negotiations with the British Government, whose interference was earnestly desired by the well-disposed of the community, a treaty was formed in the year 1816, between Rao Bharmuljee, the reigning prince, and the Bombay Government".

However, in less than three years of the British presence in Kutch, we have this report, which shows the unrest in the Kingdom. *"Invited by the principal Jareja Chiefs. A force was therefore moved against the Rao in 1819; he was deposed, and his son, Desai, was placed in power, under a regency consisting of some of the Jareja Chiefs, aided by the British Resident; and a new Treaty (No. V) was signed on 13 October 1819. This treaty, besides renewing the provisions of former engagements, guaranteed the integrity of Kutch from foreign or domestic enemies, It secured the location of a British force in Kutch, to be paid for by that State; excluded the civil and criminal jurisdiction of the British Government from Kutch; prohibited the Rao from political correspondence with, and aggression on, other States; provided for the suppression of infanticide; and guaranteed the estates of the Bhayad and other Rajput chiefs."*

This gives colour to Kutch in 1819 and brings before our eyes the problems of infanticide, which had long troubled Kutch. But it is not just Kutch which was troubled by this practice. The infanticide of new-born girls was systemic in feudatory Rajputs in India. As soon as a female child was born *"she was hold in one hand, and a knife in the other, that any person who wanted a wife might take her now, otherwise she was immediately put to death"*. The practice of female infanticide was common among the Kutch, Gujarat, and also among the Sindh in Pakistan.

Jareja Rajput chiefs or princes were the most responsible for this practice in Kutch, as the dowry for a girl would be prohibitive and the Rajputs did not wish to give their wealth away with a bride. There was a fine imposed for

this crime but the Rao did not impose the full fine and so the practice would go on. This was not stamped out until the beginning of the 20th century.

The other practice which proved hard for the British to eliminate was sati or, as the British referred to it, suttee. This was the custom of burning widows alive on the funeral pyres of their husbands. Mrs Postans on sati *"Under the British Raj the custom of suttee was suppressed. The rajahs were called upon to support the stopping of the custom. However, the belief system with the Brahmins' exhortations as to its éclat was difficult to stop. The credible people were indoctrinated by the Brahmins into the belief system and the benefits the death of the woman with the honour it bestowed on the family was so great they supported it. Where the widow did not do this her life was reduced to a shadow. She had no place within the home. She had to remove her jewellery and could only wear white. She became a shadow. She was dependent on her family. If she was a young woman she was not allowed to remarry. Her life became quite insupportable."*

And a story, for which General Napier is famous, involves a delegation of Kutch Hindu locals approaching him and complaining about the prohibition of sati. The exact wording of his response varies somewhat in different reports, but the following version captures its essence: *"You say that it is your custom to burn widows. Very well. We also have a custom: when men burn a woman alive, we tie a rope around their necks and we hang them. Build your funeral pyre; beside it, my carpenters will build a gallows. You may follow your custom. And then we will follow ours."*

Harijan woman with her heavy all encompassing cloths

Today, you can still easily discern the Hindu widows, as they wear no jewellery and dress in predominantly white or pastel colours, lilac and pale blue being most favoured today. Even the Muslims have adopted the taking out of the jewellery, and in Dhordo you can see at a glance who are widows, as while their dress is the same they wear no jewellery, which one immediately misses. Mrs Gulbeg no longer wears her five earrings, necklace, and arm bangles. Times are changing for widows, but this greatly depends on the wealth of the family, so it is still hard for many widows who are dependent on their family

There are stories that chill the heart, where the woman has been frightened and had to be forced on the fire with pitchforks. Sometimes she was given opium so she became dazed and did not know what she was doing or what was happening to her. On the other hand, there are examples of many Ranees such at Chittorgarh in Rajasthan, where after a reversal in battle the heroic Rajput warriors put on their saffron robes and went out to a certain death, while all the household women and the Ranees (queens and princesses) chose to go to the pyre rather than be captured by the triumphant conqueror.

On some palaces you can see the handprints on the palace doorjamb. The women printed them as they passed out to commit sati. The word Sati is from Sanskrit which means good, faithful.

Goddess and memory stones

Palia, or memory stones, are built to honour the woman who has gone on to the pyre on her husband's death. I have drawn three types of Hindu memory stones.

These are long stones reminiscent of our tombstones. At the top are the two symbols, the sun on the right side, the moon on the left. The turn of the ellipse of the moon indicates at what time of the month the person died. The picture symbol represents whether the person was a sati (a woman who went to the fire) or a hero warrior or a Sadhu (a holy man). Under the carved picture at the bottom is inscribed the history of the person the stone is commemorating.

By committing sati, the woman is raised to the level of a deity or goddess and I am told that this practice is still the choice of some women in

remote areas. I do not know the authenticity of this, but the fact that it is discussed shows the belief which still exists regarding this savage act. I have drawn the goddess stone, which shows a woman's arm, which means she committed sati. As it is freshly coloured orange, it means she is still honoured by her family, and likewise the family is still receiving her blessings (staima).

Diwali is the time when the living members of her family - from the husband's and father's side only - hold a feast at her memory stone and celebrate in her honour. The celebrations take place in the evening and little lights are placed round the stone. Before the feast, the idol will be freshly painted, and is often gilded with sheets of gold leaf. Certain special foods called prasad are prepared and eaten in the woman's honour. One is chapatti mixed with jaggery (solid cane sugar); another is samosas filled with a rice preparation. Whatever the food may be, it is calculated to be just enough, as all the food must be consumed at her shrine and nothing must be left over nor taken away.

I found three pallia stones in a remote village, obviously very old as they were all tilted over to one side, but they are all clearly honoured and respected as all three are freshly painted. The other two pallia I have depicted commemorate and honour warriors, or religious men. Warrior stones are known as hero stones, as the person who died showed valour, possibly in defence of his village against bandits or fighting for his king. The young Sadhu (religious man) I have drawn in one of the illustrations holds religious Hindu symbols in his hands.

Chatri or Cenotaph

Chatris, or Cenotaphs

All Hindu communities cremate their dead
and if possible - and it is always desired - the
ashes are cast into the living goddess, the river
Ganges.

Chatris (a Hindu name meaning umbrella
and describing their general appearance)
is a graceful stone canopy on four slender
pillars, which is mostly erected by wealthy or
distinguished people such as royalty. On the
outskirts of Bhuj you will find some of the royal
chatris erected in memory of their ancestors.

This idea is borrowed from the Muslims, who
have built wonderful commemorative cenotaphs
such as the Taj Mahal.

Dhordo inhabitants, being Muslim, bury their
dead in designated ground near to the village.

The pages of history books on Kutch flow
with customs particular to Kutch and Kutchi
pageantry, state processions giving us one aspect
of this pageantry. One procession from the
Victorian era is painted as a miniature and is
on display in the Aina Mahal. The Court kept
state elephants and these splendidly caparisoned
elephants with their silver houdas are preceded
in the procession by the symbols of the royal
regalia of the Kutch royal family. The golden
fish (shown on the title page of this book)
headed the procession, followed by the lion,
then a golden Ganeshe: all are held on long
poles by men on elephant back. Next came
elephants with the King and Court. Following
are European carriages and Kathiawar horses
with red hennaed tails and manes, mounted
by soldiers wearing huge bejewelled turbans
(turbans were worn of biblical proportions,
some weighing over 15 lbs). Their beards were

265

Left: Hero stone commemorating two warriors.
Right: stone commemorating a holy man.

*Goddess stone showing the arm of the woman who has gone
to the fire. Although this stone is over a century old, you see
she is still honoured, by the fact that the orange paint has
been recently refreshed, and it is freshly guided with gold leaf
squares.*

Jaani Kaya the present bard at Dhordo village

dyed with indigo and flowed over splendid, colourful uniforms. Lines of foot soldiers in their different costumes took up the rest of the procession.

This era of regalia and pomp and circumstance has long gone with the passing of the kingdom into India, but the dress of the villagers reflected this tradition of colourful costume. And its reduced form is a living memory of this time, when the costumes illustrated the dynamics of interaction between the groups, each with its own strong statement of kinship.

At the time of my first visit in 1975, when I was first introduced to members of the Royal family and the Maharao (who was the present Maharao's father), I was told by him of the last bard of the Royal household, who had just died. His passing was lamented by the Maharao, who realized that a precious link with the ancient tradition which had endured for centuries was finally broken, and the stories would be lost.

The bardic tradition was very strong in Kutch and the bard would be trained for many years. His recital would be word-perfect. He was taught never to change a word, so that the stories coming down through the ages would be the exact history of the Royal ancestors and the kingdom.

Did anyone ever write the stories down for posterity, or record the last bard's stories? I have not found any, but what wonderful personal stories they would be, and what a different world it would conjure up in the telling! Bards would have enfolded all the folk tales and stories of the kingdom with current stories of interest to entertain the Court. I wonder what tales there would be about Dhordo?

I feel sure our village would have had stories which would have contributed much and drawn the attention of the Court: and by chance this last winter I found it was so. I just happened to paint a picture of a gentle, pensive old man who was walking alone in the village. The children seeing my painting immediately told me who he was. He is a great favourite with the children and all the adults, as he tells them the stories about their village in former times. He is indeed the last bard; his family have been the bards for the village for longer than the village can remember.

I wonder what stories he has? I am already looking forward to my next visit.

Shisha

Starting at the top, illustrations progress
through the stages of securing the mirror
the fabric and then using blanket stitch
work anticlockwise to sew down the
mirror

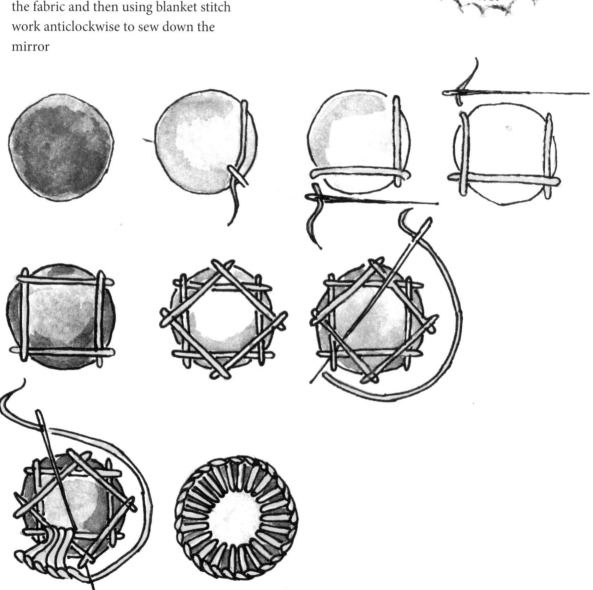

Stitches used in Banni embroidery

The illustrated stitches comprise the main stitches used in Banni embroidery. The most interesting for many embroiderers will be the sewing down of the shisha, (mirrors) and the most complex is the Maltese Cross, which in Banni they call Lace Stitch. All the other stitches are simple and will be in most ladies' repertoires. Chain stitch has many variations; I have only given the ones you will see contained in the village embroideries.

Couching

this is used to lay down the gold thread

Whipping

this is used by the Jat in their work, which makes it very rigid, as the lines are worked next to each other making a very firm solid fabric

Herringbone

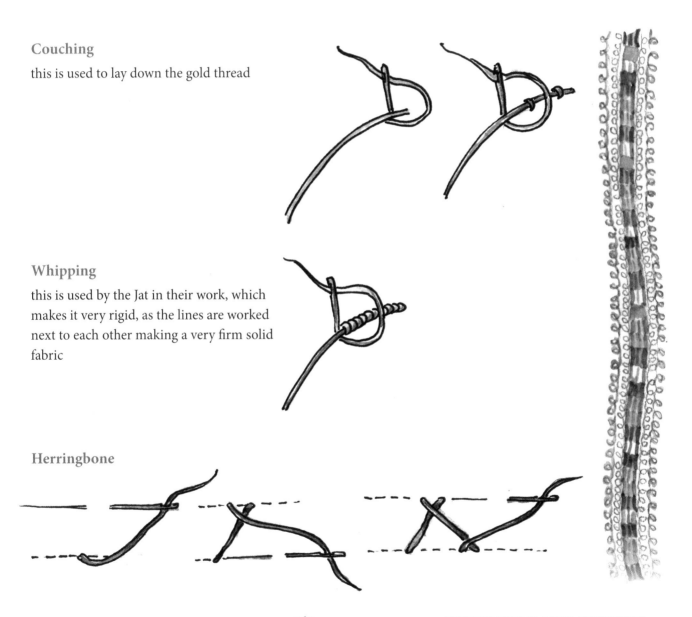

Close herringbone

used frequently making a solid line and often then embroidered with backstitch down the centre, which you can see in the illustration.

Chain stitch

Open chain

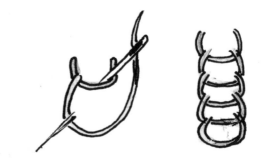

Ladder chain

Feather stitch

Double feather stitch

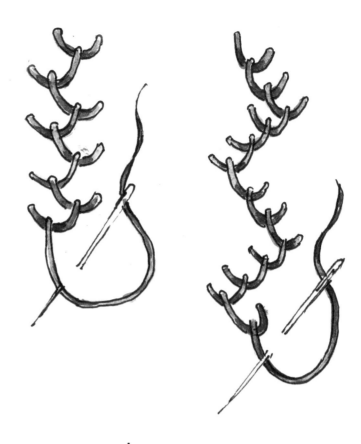

Running stitch
used to secure the layers of the quilt

Backstitch
often used to outline the motifs

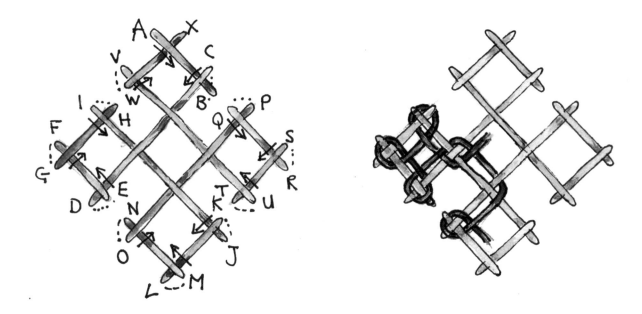

Maltese Cross

First work the interwoven latticework following the letters and direction.
Then interlace the lattice with a contrasting colour. This of course can be in
a matching colour.

Reviews

Lorna Tresidder's paintings show us a unique view of Banni in Kutch and of a way of life that is rapidly disappearing. Her deep attachment to the area and its people over more than 40 years shines through this book, which is both a visual delight and a highly informative record of a place and its culture.

Rosemary Crill

Senior Curator Asian Department, Victoria and Albert Museum, London

A superb achievement. Reading through this work of love brought back to life all I remember about Kutch in those times. The illustrations are beautifully fresh and spontaneous and take you on a rich visual journey page after page. The living tradition of embroidery is manifest in the daily life and culture of this region.

Joss Graham

Ethnographic Textiles and Works of Art, London

Lorna's repeated visits to Kutch has culminated in the impressive book she has produced, and shows clearly the distinctive dress that each group wore at the time of her first visit in 1975, when I was the District Development Officer for Kutch. I had the privilege of organising her visits to the many artisans in Textiles and Embroidery and to visit the various and often remote and nomadic groups of people. The book will go a long way to enriching our knowledge of the culture and mores of the Kutchese and in particular the villages in the Banni area.

A Prasad

IAS Officer Retired as Additional Secretary to the Government of Gujarat Gandhinagar

I have known Lorna Tresidder for 30 years and during her many visits she has observed and studied the culture of the people of this region. Her book 'The Golden Thread' with her beautiful illustrations and writing, truly express the life of the Kutchi people. It is a unique, interesting and lovely book; and a timely record of this disappearing way of life.

Pramod Jethi

Curator, Aina Mahal Museum, Bhuj

Lorna Tresidder is an artist and writer with an acute perceptive eye, writing about the Banni villages and the demise of their culture since 1975. A major attraction of the book are the excellent landscapes and beautiful portraits which vividly bring these people to life, in this once remote area of Kutch.

Carmen Kagal

Editor of many books on Indian Art, Mumbai

The dedication and love she has for the Banni people since the seventies and up to the present day shine through in her paintings and writing. We have so many books on Kutch but Lorna by her paintings shows a much more in-depth vivid view. Indeed her textiles seem more authentic than photographs. The book takes us back to those days which are now gone and which we used to see earlier – a unique and timely record of our vanished culture.

Abubaker Wazir

Collector of Indian Textiles, Bhuj